Distance Becomes Communion

A DOMINICAN SYMPOSIUM
ON MISSION AND HOPE

Edited by
Geraldine Smyth OP

DOMINICAN PUBLICATIONS

First published (2004) by
Dominican Publications
42 Parnell Square
Dublin 1

ISBN 1-871552-86-9

British Library Cataloguing in Publications Data.
A catalogue record for this book is available
from the British Library.

Cover design by Bill Bolger

Printed in Ireland by
The Leinster Leader Ltd
Naas, Co. Kildare.

Contents

Preface

The occasion of this volume was a symposium of five Congregations of Dominican Sisters from the United States, Australia and New Zealand, invited by the Dominican Sisters in Ireland (Cabra Congregation) the 'mother-root' from which they had sprung. From 1860 onwards, the founding Irish sisters from the Dominican communities of Cabra, Sion Hill and Kingstown-Dun Laoghaire, had volunteered for the new missions in Louisiana, Australia and New Zealand, contemporaneous with others who would also leave Cabra and Sion Hill for the foundations in South Africa's Western and Eastern Cape. All were part of the missionary *diaspora* of the period. The symposium in Ireland, 2nd to 8th August, 2003 – the first-ever coming together of these Congregations – took as its theme, 'From Threads to Tapestry: a Dominican Journey in Mission and Hope'.

It was the great Jubilee celebrated by Christians across the world in the year 2000 which inspired the Congregation Council of the Dominican Congregation (Cabra, Ireland) to invite the five independent Congregations, 'descended' from the first and subsequent groups of Dominicans, who, from 1860 onwards, had set sail from Dun Laoghaire Harbour or Dublin Port. The invitation found a response, as immediate as it was enthusiastic, particularly to that echo from the biblical Jubilee tradition that called for a return to the ancestral home, for a time of rejoicing and renewal. In short, the dialogue took wings, with memory and imagination – in the lovely phrase of T. S. Eliot – 'stirring dull roots with spring rain.' Soon, plans formed for reverse journeys back to Ireland: not as a voyage into nostalgia, but as a pilgrimage linked by a shared memory and hope. The impulse was a desire to bring to life the unspoken or half-forgotten stories and shrouded histories, and to create a space for that story-forming narrative to open up, perhaps, new possibilities of solidarity in our Dominican charism and mission.

Over three years of real and 'virtual' conversations, the plans were laid: the Consultors' Group corresponded, designing and weaving together the different strands of the symposium, ensuring an interplay of internal narrative and critical reflection: speakers and respondents, liturgists and artists, archivists and annalists, formal lectures and visits beyond the meeting place at Tallaght to pilgrim sites of the Celtic Christian and Dominican past. Some of these, like St Dominic's Well in Esker, Galway, or the monastic site of Glendalough in Wicklow, continue to appeal to the contemporary religious imagination. The decision at the inter-congregational planning-meeting in Rome 2001 was for predominantly Irish-based 'main speakers', with responses and homilies provided by the visitors, ensuring an intercultural mix and mutual enrichment. There were sixty-one participants, but access to open lectures, public events and exhibitions, together with seminars hosted by the original 'sending communities', extended the scope of the symposium.

The public significance was visible in opening contributions from visiting dignitaries. Tributes were paid by Dr John Herron, Australian Ambassador to Ireland, and Mr Alan McCarthy, Honorary New Zealand Consul, each embracing the opportunity to acknowledge the astonishing vision and achievement of Dominican Sisters in their respective countries, especially in the fields of education, social justice and intercultural reconciliation. The symbolic presence of Captain Jim Carter, Dun Laoghaire Harbour Master, lent a maritime outlook on the scale of the risk and courage of those women pioneers, who, more than a hundred and forty years before, had braved long, perilous voyages to earth's ends, and in those post-famine decades accompanied thousands of their country-women and countrymen into exile, whether driven by poverty or the search for a better life. Captain Carter also commented upon the unbroken dedication of the Dominican Convent in the social history of Kingstown-Dun Laoghaire. He paid tribute too to the Dominicans who remained on in the convent overlooking the harbour, to become widely recognized as the anchor of educational life in the town for generations of young people down to the present. Bishop Colm O'Reilly (representative of the Irish Episcopal Conference to the Irish Missionary Union) added his voice in celebration of the many missionaries from Ireland who went out and made their home among other people and cultures, but who also received so much back, that many made the ultimate choice, asking that their bones be laid to rest in the lands that had welcomed them.

This book comprises three parts: the first consisting of five chapters from the Irish-based contributors, invited because of their knowledge and experience in various intersecting fields – history, theology, women's studies, missiology, and ecumenics – and presented here in the original sequence. The second part brings together a rich sample of responses from 'overseas' speakers – Sisters Carmel Walsh (Aotearoa-New Zealand), Edmund Gibson and Mary Daniel (New Orleans), Angela Moloney (South Australia), Regina O'Neill (Western Australia) and Rosemary Lewins and Elizabeth Hellwig (Eastern Australia and the Solomon Islands) – which strike home in the manner of living narrative or historical case study, and which together with the homily texts of Sisters Margaret Scharf (Western Australia) and Judith Lawson (Eastern Australia) in part three, give a sense of vital immediacy and inter-cultural texture of faith as it has been embodied and handed on in lives often stranger than fiction. These texts invite us to take off our shoes. They leave us by turns humbled and amazed.

Geraldine Smyth, O.P., sets a context for the symposium in Chapter 1 – 'Spanning the Distance: Dominican Mission Connecting Global and Local'. She offers a reflection on the contemporary global challenge of discovering unity in diversity across the intersections of time and space. The central concern here is to recognize the changing 'place' of mission and to explore the impact of globalization 'from above' and 'from below', together with the recent ethnic upsurges and identity politics that cut across the more historically constructed boundaries between nation and nation. The quest for a new mission paradigm must reckon with a world and Church that are incorrigibly plural, de-centred and open to the Reign of God within history; yet available when times demand, to posit a subversive critique of powers that oppress, and to 'brush against the grain of history'. Dominicans are called to connect the diverse richness of their tradition of contemplating and preaching the Gospel in vastly differing contexts, eager to share gifts and burdens, collaborating in creating a 'new catholicity' – through concerted engagement in contemplation, action and reflection.

Margaret MacCurtain, O.P., in Chapter 2, 'Tending the Wells of Memory – Sharing Sources of Hope', asserts the emergent significance of women's history, especially under the impulse of feminist scholarship, of women as agents of their own history both in Church and society. In the creative metaphor of tending the wells of memory, she offers an alternative construal of the Irish missionary *diaspora*, premised on the insight that those nineteenth century Dominican missionary women were motivated primarily by a gospel desire to follow their people into exile, and, later by a passion for justice, collaborating with those peoples already there, in causes of right and truth. She prises open new meanings within the shared memory of famine, *diaspora*, or assimilation, indicating the choices available as we reciprocate knowledge and experience in the struggle for equality and liberation in a world where hope must rise to meet the challenges of multiculturalism and global responsibility.

In Chapter 3, Anne Thurston situates the enterprise of historic retrieval in the context of ground-breaking research by biblical scholars and theologians. Demonstrating the contemporary hermeneutical shift within the discourse of biblical interpretation of so many 'valiant women', her own reading of the texts of Miriam and Mary of Magdala enhance the critical project of bringing women 'out of the shadows'. In exploring the dubious reasons and controlling interests which have contributed to the exclusion of women from the exercise of their prophetic vocation and from being witnesses to the Resurrection, she deftly picks up the broken threads that connect the 'then' of history to the 'now' of faith, attesting that the biblical tapestry of 'valiant women' still survives as an irrepressible memory and a living Word in the subversive reach of Christian hope.

An Australian-born theologian of Irish descent, living and working in Ireland for over fifteen years, John D'Arcy May, in Chapter 4, brings a unique insider-outsider perspective. He views the changing face of mission from the era of colonial conquest to that in which Western capitalism entraps the vast majority of the world's citizens in systems of human degradation and economic misery. With the apt theme, 'The Space In Between: Mission as Reconciliation' he explores mission in the contemporary Church and world, challenging the arrogance of eurocentric forms of mission. He probes them sensitively, cautioning against false understandings of mission aimed at conversion by coercion, and, equally, the inadequacy of measuring the effectiveness of mission in terms of successful development, relief work or institutional projects of health care or education. Mission in the post-modern world occurs in the interstices of the global system, creating spaces in which strangers can meet, and reconciliation becomes possible through forgiveness, healing and restitution.

Mary O'Driscoll, O.P., has been an itinerant preacher and teacher on every continent, teasing out with others in their particular contexts, the rich diversity of the Dominican charism. In Chapter 5, 'The Dominican Vision: "A Passion of Possibility"' she plays upon a vision of Kierkegaard, as a lens through which to ponder the founding dream of Dominic, rooted in God's 'passion for the possible'. She advances exciting historical exemplars of women preachers of truth, showing that from the outset, Dominic included them alongside the friars and lay companions, as integral to the 'communities of holy preaching' around which his Order was constituted. Catherine of Siena is no exceptional case. Forgotten name after forgotten name is lifted up and affirmed – from Margaret Ebner and other Rhineland women of the fourteenth century, to Rose, 'Mother of the Poor' in Peru, to the two seventeenth century Catherines who conducted study circles in the mountains of China, to the Irish Dominican foremothers, Julian Nolan and Mary Lynch who came back in their advanced years (from long exile in an enclosed Spanish monastery) to restore women's Dominican life in Ireland in 1686. Such archetypal women stand as inspiration to Dominican women and to other communities of faith. This vision belongs to them, inviting them to 'a humble intelligence of the heart' in exercising their charism as preachers and peacemakers in a broken world.

Until this symposium, the stories of those other valiant women who departed Ireland in the 1860s, existed as two halves of a tapestry: in the new places of mission – USA, Australia, New Zealand, and in the 'home-mission' in Ireland, where in 1928 the Irish Dominican communities had formed an amalgamation under the Cabra motherhouse. (The South African sisters augmented that amalgamation by formally re-grafting onto the mother-root [1938], followed by the community in Portugal [1955], and by Galway with its newly founded mission-community in Argentina [1969]; the Brazil mission would emerge in 1991 out of a cross-congregational collaboration of sisters from Portugal, Ireland and South Africa.) Sr Maureen MacMahon's *logo* portrays a ship turned vigorously into the waves, its rigging and sails suggesting the artist's vision of the rich tapestry of Dominican missionary lives woven under the breath of the Spirit. Threads flying the wind invite the idea of broken strands seeking others to be woven into new patterns. For indeed, the distances that divided those first missionary women – and those later native-born and Irish sisters as would later join them – were so vast as to make sustained communication impossible. Such narratives as existed in diary and letter often lay buried in annals and archives, to be recovered perhaps a century later. But oral remnants survived, and memories revivified through occasional meetings of individuals, or correspondence arising from an archivist's query, or (post Vatican II, as home-leave became possible) through passing visits of erstwhile pupils with former teachers. The re-discovery of these connections has sparked a new consciousness that these stories live on; that histories can be reclaimed and still have the power to inspire communion of faith and hope. These find new expression in the second part of the book, where, after a hundred and forty years, the two halves of the tapestry come together.

It remains to thank those sisters of the Consultors' Group who worked indefatigably in the preparation and celebration of this first Dominican Symposium, Srs Caitríona Geraghty, Rose O'Neill, Máire Kealy, Monica Devers, Dominique Horgan and Maura Duggan, and not least my own community and Congregation council: Srs Elizabeth Healy, Francis Krige, Veronica Mc Cabe and Mary O'Driscoll. Warm appreciation go out also to the Prioresses and Sisters of the Dominican Congregation of Eastern Australia and the Solomon Islands; the Dominican Congregation of Aotearoa-New Zealand; the Dominican Sisters of Western Australia; the Dominican Congregation of the Holy Cross South Australia, and the Dominican Congregation of St Mary New Orleans for their commitment and for travelling so far. Without such partnership and fidelity to the vision, it could never have become reality. We owe gratitude to our Dominican brothers – the Prior Provincial, and local Prior and community – for their hospitality and liturgical support; as well as to the Director and friendly staff of the Retreat Centre, who catered for every human need; I acknowledge also our contemplative Sisters in Siena Convent, Drogheda, who although absent, were united in spirit, sustaining the endeavour in prayer. Particular thanks go to the unnamed artists in all our Congregations who designed and stitched the beautiful historic panels as an expression of a common history and future hope. These are included within the pages of this book. I trust I will be indulged in naming the artists – Srs Monica Devers, Helen McGing, Patrice de Burgh and Clare Donnelly – whose work in the Celtic tradition features in Bill Bolger's fine cover-design: the cosmos still in the process of becoming, the vivid interactions and colours of natural landscape and animal husbandry; the salmon of wisdom caught on a golden line, as it rises towards the Trinity knot reminiscent of illuminated Gospel manuscripts and intimating a shared ministry of education; the shield-like discs representing the Dominican motto – *Laudare, Benedicere, Praedicare;* and the Atlantic Wild Geese, emblematic of our missionaries who journeyed to South Africa, Australia, Aotearoa-New Zealand, Louisiana and Latin America.

Thanks are due to Deirdre O'Dwyer for her extensive and calm administrative support and to Fr Bernard Treacy, O.P., of Dominican Publications for his wise oversight of the publication, ensuring that the texts gain access to a wider interested readership. The rest is yet to be. Future prospects lie within the vision of God and in the indomitable spirit of the sisters at the symposium who, in the final seminar, pledged themselves to stay together. Distance becomes communion. Seamus Heaney observes that any given inheritance can always be reimagined. Having disclosed to one another during an outstanding week the newness in our heritage; having 're-found' one another, now under the wind of the Spirit and Sustainer of all life and mission, we dare to make new designs on mission.

The book is dedicated to the memory of three valiant missionary women: Sisters Declan Callaly (Western Australia), Jerome Keary (Cabra Congregation) and Mary Therese Sweeney (South Australia), who died in the days just prior to the symposium, and to the many who went before them. We remember these pilgrim sisters who keep before us the ultimate horizon of all mission in the *missio Dei Trinitatis*, and pray the final cadence of that ninth-century Marian hymn, *Ave Maris Stella*, beloved of travellers worldwide, as we entrust them to the God of journeys, the God of sea and ocean who goes before us and looks out for our coming home: 'May our hope find harbour in the calm of Jesus.'

Geraldine Smyth OP

Feast of St Albert the Great
15 November 2003

Spanning the Distance – Dominican Mission Global and Local

GERALDINE SMYTH, O.P.

UNITY-IN-DIVERSITY: A MATTER OF SPACE

The lyrics of the Nanci Griffith song, 'From a Distance', evoke the paradox of a world shattered by the clamour of war and the silent scream of famine. For human creatures reflecting on this world from the perspective of one watching 'from a distance', an image of a God of remote freedom comes into view, one impervious to the pathos of the world. We have also come to appreciate the irony that, however our vast world may have diminished to whatever image of the global life-space or to whatever capacity for information to spin around it in seconds, it will take something of a different order than technology, for communication to lead to community. It will require a different kind of vision to apprehend God's watching us from beyond the terrifying 'infinite spaces', as with face bent in caring providence and compassion.

Language and culture are changing in step with this new consciousness of space. In industrialized countries, we hear talk of needing personal space, and of boundaries to keep others from 'invading our space'. We have come to see 'space' as the condition of well-being. Before, we had no time; now, we have no space. In the open space technology of the market, people under pressure speak of 'claiming their space,' and space (as much as time) is a marketable commodity. Books on Feng Shui are all the rage, gurus assuring us that clearing out our closets will open up our souls. Lifestyle revision 'retreats' and wilderness experiences are now big business. Clarifying our life-space is cultivated to an art-form, an antidote to our getting and spending, offering (temporary) respite from personal stress, urban sprawl and social displacement.

A marked feature of contemporary city life is the disappearance of public space with its architecture of civic meeting-places where strangers and natives could mingle at ease.[1] In non-industrialized countries, one impact of globalization has been the cultural uprooting of communities in the search for work, and consequent erosion of viable local spaces of culture and economy with their sustaining social and spiritual networks. The rapacious arm of multinational agribusiness has likewise ravaged eco-systems that are aeons old, and polluted habitable space for present and future generations of long-inculturated communities.[2]

This transformed 'consciousness of space' then, also involves a 'spatialization of consciousness'[3] which carries an inherent ambivalence. This ambivalence turns on the vexed relationship of the one and the many, the universal and the particular, and the dialectical possibility of unity in diversity. In theological terms, we can relate this ambivalence, and indeed paradox, to God's transcendence and utter freedom and to God's immanence and incarnate love present within creation. A characteristic spatial image of the twentieth century is the 'concentration camp' with contemporary variations nowadays in the refugee camps to be found in all our countries. We need to draw from our spiritual and theological traditions, counter spatial images, such as 'garden' as place of creation and blessing (Gen 2:10-16), the garden of resurrection or new creation (Jn 20:11ff.); 'Jerusalem as the city of peace' (Rev 21:2ff.)[4] or the world itself, as 'sanctuary' (Gen 7-8; Is 11:9).[5] Such symbols may give rise to new reflections on space that reconnect us to the domain of God's creation in terms that express life in all its diversity as interrelational, dynamic and revelatory of the mystery of God, hidden and present.

Ecclesiologically, this new understanding of space can also be correlated to the Church's call to be generously universal *and* intensely local in its expression of vision, solidarity and justice. Thus, the mystery imbuing the view of the world from space, the sense of awe that its vision evoked in the first astronauts, somehow symbolizes the possibility of a worldview that has some sense of wholeness, but without aspiration to the rationalist 'view-of-everything-from-nowhere', and the illusion of the value-free paradigm which has so dominated recent centuries. But – and here the paradox – this new understanding, linked to the shared view of the world from space, somehow discloses that the distance, which separates one person or country from another, may be traversed; boundaries that divide nations, cultures and faiths may – however fleetingly – be transcended, and those once strangers may find a common ground. So – and still the paradox – the sense of the local is also changed. The 'return' to the local is not only by a different route, but travels, necessarily, via other local places, and signposts a necessary interdependence of parts and whole.[6]

Put differently, two interrelated possibilities become clear: that of holding open a space for the local in its vibrant cultural values, bonds and expressions of shared life, but liberated from claims of blood and soil, or from a 'privatising' of public space; and, on the other hand, the possibility of the wider vision of the universal, but liberated from the pull into context-less abstraction that would overwhelm the particularities of local religion and culture, refusing any *actual* encounter with the human face and with the face of the earth in their concrete otherness.

It is worth noting that Robert Schreiter, whose groundbreaking work on mission and inculturation in the 1980s brought us back to the local and to respect for local culture as a necessary entry-point in mission,[7] in his subsequent work, went on to grapple with the reality that cultures do come into conflict; here he asserted the necessary possibilities of dialogue *between* cultures, and an engaged practice of reconciliation.[8] Still more recently, Schreiter, taking both negative and positive account of the realities of globalization, has called for a retrieval and renewal of those universal and catholic dimensions in our relations within our world home.[9]

UNITY-IN-DIVERSITY: A MATTER OF TIME

The intuition of a new catholicity and of the expanding potential to affirm newfound links across the *space* of God's creation, intimates one aspect of the inspiration and risk behind this symposium. Another relates to our deepening sense as Dominicans, and specifically as Dominican women, of the interconnections in our history: both solidarity in our shared story, and concern that so much of that history has remained untold.

In recent decades, there has been a recovery of the category of narrative as a way of understanding the temporal paradoxes of identity, and offering a rich vein of insight into the dynamic narratives which shape our sense of meaning, belonging and social being.[10] It has been thanks also to a reawakened consciousness of how our all our stories are threaded into the whole divine narrative of creation, salvation and sanctification, that religious women have been motivated to articulate their particular story as something to be remembered and celebrated. This has also alerted us to the profound kinship between memory and hope – once described by John Baptist Metz as the twin impulses of the human condition. Margaret MacCurtain shares important insights on the significance of the recent flourishing of women's writing in general, and of the abundance of narrative emerging from congregations of religious women, in particular. Interestingly, it should be said, still another inspiration behind this symposium, has been the emergence of a 'community' of Dominican story-makers across the congregations represented here, and of the relationship of hospitality, solidarity and exchange between them, that has prompted a new recollection of the truth that historical 'digging' is not a task of nostalgia, but an exercise in memory and imagination. Imagination is memory's offspring.

And so another connection was sensed between an old mission-story that needed to be told in all our hearing – in the presence of the 'descendants' of those who went out from Ireland in the 1860s and in subsequent waves, and simultaneously in the hearing and presence of the 'descendants' of those Dominican sisters from whom they departed, in Cabra, Sion Hill, Dun Laoghaire and the other Dominican communities in Ireland, which eventually amalgamated in 1928 to form one Congregation, and into which, the kindred Dominican Sisters in South Africa, Portugal and Galway in due course re-conjoined. [11]

Buried connections and analogies have been uncovered between those times and places long distant, when the first groups of Dominican women set out from Irish shores, in the main never to return, making their life in far-flung places; and our contemporary time and place in a global world that is still fraught with risk, where mission is being constrained by different kinds of limits and urgent challenges, and where, once more, the sources of imagination are stirred, travellers on inverse journeys come onto the horizon, and subversive networks of solidarity come to be woven.

Since Einstein, we have come to see our world in terms of a space-time continuum that transcends previously-conceived notions of matter as monolithic and static, space as empty, and time as either linear or cyclical. Julia Kristeva, commenting on the second generation of feminist theorists, posited the need for other understandings of time, capable of bringing together the concerns of time and place. She proposed a model that included and transcended the interests of the self, one that took bodily narratives seriously, while insisting on the need to make space for 'otherness' within those narratives. (Anne Thurston clearly demonstrates how Miriam's place in the biblical tradition was achieved because of those who refused, over the centuries, to allow her memory to be suppressed, and who resisted the attempts to collapse her vocation and her story into those of her brother, Moses.)

Kristeva coined the phrase 'Maternal Time', pointing to the reality of birth as the radical symbol of letting go to the other through a willingness to make bodily space within oneself to be inhabited by new life; in due time, to suffer a rupture in one's very being, and in the birth event to allow the separation necessary for an altogether new way of relationship. This 'Maternal Time', construed as taking on a kind of death in one's body (a giving up of any claim to one's own identity as all-absorbing or totalizing), is presented as an invitation to re-imagine identity as both radically other *and* radically relational. 'Maternal Time' is thus presented as an alternative to violence – with its logic of 'a fight to the death'. This 'fight to the death' is exemplified repeatedly in linear time as one identity contests with another, playing out a history of winners and losers, of victors and vanquished.[12]

Pondering this model, it is not difficult to find a certain resonance with the Christian understanding of communion, grounded in the Eucharist as the living memory (*anamnesis*) of Christ's sacrificial self-offering (*kenosis*). Through such voluntary laying down and ceding over his life that others may live, salvation is made possible in ways that embody life, healing and inclusive relationship, which hold open a hope beyond human desert or control, and a future that refuses to be determined by the past with its recurring pattern of suffering, sin and mortality. This bid to overcome the mechanisms of linear time with its relentless cycle of victory and defeat finds its positive correlative in a communion (*koinonia*) – however fragile – grounded in memory and history, but bearing the promise of hope that will be fulfilled in the eschatological banquet of the coming Reign of God.[13]

RE-CONNECTING SPACE AND TIME, MEMORY AND HOPE

Elsewhere in this volume, John D'Arcy May interprets the colonial enterprise and its influence on Christian understandings of mission, not through the time-honoured approach of a historic imperative with its related notions of manifest destiny, but through the lens of 'space', appealing to the ancient soul-maps as much as to historic geography of colonialism with its maps of the carving up of conquered territory.[14] Although religious legitimization frequently bolstered the colonial claims of the inevitability of 'historic progress', many now acknowledge that the rampant cultural depredation in so many colonized places, rather than making history, was an exercise of massive disruption that could be more aptly described as 'history-stopping.'[15] This is the place for tears, for rituals of repentance and the concerted practice of reparation.

Mission finds a focus in the interplay of memory and imagination – with hope as its third partner – conspiring towards a space for meeting, in which to seek connections both original and strange. In the Jubilee tradition of returning to the ancestral home, all – both hosts and guests – take off their shoes, prepared for humble encounter, remembering with T.S. Eliot, that 'at every meeting we are meeting a stranger.'[16]

And yet, those daring journeys of the first founding women, inspired by a vision of preaching the Gospel in far-off lands, are somehow paradigmatic for us. The *diaspora* of mission that developed in the subsequent hundred and forty years embraced many hundreds more women in an ongoing pilgrimage. Those who have now returned do so not simply as to the aboriginal place of their founders. Their homecoming somehow constitutes a reversal, offering sacred space (*temenos*) within whose circle the stories can be heard and shared with those who are at once friends and strangers. Unlike those who sailed out of Irish harbours on journeys that took them Westward to Louisiana, or Southbound to the Eastern or Western Cape, to

Eastern and Southern Australia, to Aotearoa-New Zealand and thence to Western Australia, the symposium participants have steered a reverse direction – have come 'back East', or travelled the long haul North to the place that Ireland's emigrants call 'the old country'. This is not so much a wheel coming full circle, but recalls rather the spiralling design of Celtic loop, or an Indigenous ritual of the 'Dreamtime' that followed ancient 'Songlines' in a hidden, unifying pattern, returning life back to the earth while opening to the heavens. Standing in the stream of this tradition, we acknowledge the ancient harmonies and respond to the call to weave new and different textures in the tapestry, making new and other 'designs' on mission.

MISSION – A JUBILEE-INSPIRED VISION AND RESPONSIBILITY
We have already suggested the correlation between the symposium and the Jubilee – that, perhaps u-topian, event from the Judaeo-Christian tradition. Celebrated every seven years, it was a way of heralding a great transformation of cosmic, social and spiritual proportions; through its reversals, the rhythm of life found its equilibrium restored, with a healing of fractured human relations. Through turning aside from the daily drive of work and routine to welcome the life of the Spirit and those on the outer edges of the community, God's people could celebrate God's blessings, drawing strength from one another in reorienting their lives to the pattern of the covenant and the *missio Dei*.

There is a way of seeing Jubilee as a space which the community allowed periodically, to create a new balance of care and justice and joy – among family, kin and stranger – or indeed any who had been neglected, mistreated or even justly punished. Debts would be cancelled, prisoners released, in a year-long Sabbath – to let the earth lie fallow, to give everyone time enough to make their way, from wherever their journey had brought them, back to the home of their ancestors (Lev 25). There was the matching expectation that they would find a great welcome, a space of hospitality and thanksgiving. Perhaps, Robert Frost was inspired by this collective memory when he mused that home is where if you've got to go there, they've got to take you in.

And so in the interplay of memory and imagination there emerges an implicit hope in Dominican mission today as still evoking the dreams and responsibility of Dominican women, called to be preachers of truth in our contemporary world. In Paul Ricoeur's apt phrasing, in opening to the story 'behind the text' of our common history, there is a conviction of a life 'in front of the text', waiting to be engaged,[17] even as the current of the Spirit stirs through the loose, uneven threads, moving the imagination with new symbols, and with the urge to go and tell – like Mary of Magdala, as depicted in Anne Thurston's portrayal – to go and tell the good news of life, death and resurrection at work in our life-contexts, to go and share the story, in word, craft, music and liturgy. In undertaking to become pilgrims together as Dominican Sisters finding a new dimension of communion within the worldwide Dominican Family, we are ready to re-discover what it means to be partners in the divine mission, part of the mysterious trinitarian movement of outpouring and returning (exitus and reditus), as envisioned by Thomas Aquinas and by Meister Eckhart, at one in God and with one another, and responsive to the needs of our ecumenical world-home.

LOCATING OURSELVES IN THE NEW WORLD ORDER

Any inquiry into what Dominican mission as a project of communion and solidarity might mean in a global context, must now take account of the realities of a world increasingly driven by globalization – however contested the meaning and extent of those realities – but also of the changing context of the geo-political world order, and the rapidity with which that order is being redefined. However aware we may be that these are not merely a static back-drop to our mission, we must also take account of how our (largely Western) presuppositions structure our world view. Our position shapes what we see: whether that be on the crest of the Northern Atlantic wave or poised on the Pacific Rim, with easy access to the most prized global goods – information, knowledge, money, power, food-security, clean water, human rights; or whether we live on the underside of history among the Poor and the 'non-persons' of this world. Location affects vision, and so we need to 'look twice' in order to become critically conscious of our privileged stance, of the partiality of our viewpoint, and of whom and what it excludes. We must be ready, as the Jewish philosopher, Walter Benjamin challenged, 'to brush against the grain' of our cultural history and its conditioning.[18]

Even when living close to the 'non-persons' of history, one may remain still unaware of the reality of the Poor in *other* contexts whose plight or concerns may be different. Those who can view the world from the window of aeroplane or automobile and can satisfy their wants by waving the magic wand of the plastic card, falter in their effort to imagine a table bare of food day in day out, know nothing of what it is to be submerged in destitution, and cannot – without some displacement – find ways of solidarity with those in their millions who are abandoned to the labyrinthine injustice of international debt, or barred access to simple patented medicines. Again, Benjamin paints a graphic picture of how power, wielded by history's winners, also makes them blind to its victims: Thus, 'empathy with the victor invariably benefits the ruler [who] in the triumphal procession … steps over those who are lying prostrate.'[19]

Furthermore, it behoves us to remember that all our Western bias is towards perceiving the world through human eyes and ears, with scant reference to the effects of globalization on the fragile ecology of the animal and plant world, and of the planet at large. Here, our Indigenous sisters and brothers have much to teach us if we would listen.[20]

It is necessary that the very systems of globalization be de-mystified, probed, and subverted by means of a 'globalizaion from below' in actions countervailing to the 'globalization from above', towards practice of ethical democracy and global civil society?[21] Richard Falk argues that such 'globalization-from-below' can be developed along lines of 'an embedded consensus' with eight practical and practicable elements, including, for example, consent of citizenry, human rights, participation, accountability and non-violence.[22]

Bearing this in mind and endeavouring to be critically aware of how our political, social and economic location pre-conditions our world-view, it may be helpful to outline further some of the salient challenges of our 'globalized' world, with reference to Christian mission within and across different cultures. It is now commonplace to date the seismic shifts in the global order to September 11, 2001, following the devastating attacks by Al Q'aeda on United States soil, and linked to the consequent bombing and occupation of Iraq by the United States and Britain. But, it is arguable that tectonic shifts in inter-national relations had already begun in 1989 with the (relatively non-violent) collapse of the Berlin Wall.

THE CHANGING SPACE OF GLOBALIZATION

As the 1990s turned into the twenty-first century, 'globalization' was the watchword denoting both our over-arching context and the kind of world we are in.[23] There seems little that is *not* ascribed to its smothering interlocking embrace. Thus, mass communication and travel – with its time-space compression and resultant erosion of local space, culture, and identity – polarize even as they purport to equalize and unite.[24] Protectionist global market protocols throw up road-blocks against poorer countries struggling desperately to trade their way into the global system, but the collapse of their agricultural and manufacturing base is rendered inevitable by 'the powers that be' and by 'the way things are.'[25] Self-propelling financial markets operate ruthlessly against such countries. In the closing days of 2001, we witnessed something of globalization as a vicious economic circle, when the weak *rouble* collapsed in Russia; almost instantly, reverberations were felt in Argentina where the *peso* went into free-fall. The scale of protest was unprecedented as even those hitherto un-buffeted by financial hardship milled onto the streets in tens of thousands. In quick succession, a number of governments resigned. Several other countries were caught in the domino effect, South Africa in particular. There the value of the *rand* plummeted, in turn undermining virtually every sub-Saharan African economy in a matter of days.

Since the ending of the Cold War, the old paradigm of international relations based on nuclear deterrence with its balance of enmity between Western and Eastern powers has fractured, with new alignments of power emerging. Doubtless, these have been twisted into further new shapes since 2001. One of the main instruments for global governance – the United Nations – has suffered severe blows, as the United States, moved by the threat or fear of global terrorism, has adopted unilateralist moral, political and military stances in the world arena. In the recent past, we have heard in almost apocalyptic terms a new discourse that would split the world's nations into opposing camps, ascribing them to 'the axis of evil', or 'the alliance of the willing', according to their putative tolerance of (however passive) or resistance (prescriptively active) to 'global terrorism'. Dissenting voices, however, have not been lacking among nations and global organizations such as the U.N., as well as among Churches and religious bodies, protesting against such rigidly affixed identities and predetermined international policies, thankfully breaking up the fearful symmetry of a new map of the world based on the 'clash of civilisations' theory.[26]

One must be wary of this seduction, by which Samuel Huntington contests that the wars of this century will be fought not on the basis of a conflict of ideology (liberal capitalism *versus* fascism or communism, as in the past), but on a clash of cultural identities or 'civilisations' – with the Arab-Muslim and Western-Christian 'civilisations' being presented as the main antagonists. It is necessary that thinking people resist the smooth fallacy that Arab-Muslims and Western-Christians can be thus marshalled into monolithic blocs, without reference to the manifest pluralism within political traditions and religious traditions, East and West, and to developments in inter-faith dialogue,[27] not to mention the evidence of the cultural deformations of religion in *many* religious, geographical and historical contexts. One must also acknowledge the increasingly multicultural nature of our societies, with the inherent *potential* of enriching inter-cultural exchange.

Certainly too, there is a challenge to Christian theology to probe its own tradition for the recurring instances of ideological distortions that betray the biblical call to welcome the stranger (Ex 23:9) and to forgive enemies (Mt 6:12; Lk 6: 32-38)).[28] The ideology of apartheid, for example, was given legitimacy with biblical and theological arguments from some South African Churches, and had to be tackled on those grounds by prophetic theologians within the offending Christian tradition.[29]

THE CHANGING FACE OF MISSION

For us as Dominicans, there are also implications arising from our charism about searching out new expressions of truth both in familiar contexts and in 'other' locations, and about engaging in cross-cultural dialogue as we seek to build a global ethic of justice and peace. In these pursuits, it will be necessary to keep submitting our assumptions and practices to critical reflection. In more positive terms, we are called to reflect afresh on what catholicity might mean in this new world order, and to explore new ways of bringing together the local and the global, for the sake of the gospel imperatives of truth and justice, liberation, and peace. Are we not also called to build together on what we discover: to *ex-pose* (open a space) for the cries of the poor and the groaning of creation; to be communities of hope within the wider *oikoumene*, catholic in the sense of the whole Church present as 'all in each place'; in solidarity with one another in union with Christ who is our 'all in all'? It is to this diverse, ecumenical oneness that we as Church are called to be the sign and sacrament in our world, called together with other Churches and people of good will, to live a 'new catholicity.'

MISSION WITHIN A NEW CATHOLICITY:
'GLOBAL THEOLOGICAL FLOWS'

Robert Schreiter has pointed to a number of practical ways in which this new catholicity can be enacted in terms that should appeal to the customary Dominican conviction that theology must correlate philosophical and social analysis and reflection with gospel *praxis* and vision. This means holding in creative tension the modes and dynamics of reason (open intellectual searching), experience (including bodily, emotional, spiritual social, political), and revelation – including the interpretative process within the community of the tradition, that living stream into which we have been baptised, the community of 'all in each place'.[30]

In giving substance to the 'new catholicity', Schreiter has identified four thematic *movements* – 'global theological flows'. These are: theology of liberation, feminist theologies, theologies of ecology and, theologies of human rights. He goes on to demonstrate how these have functioned with both vitality (at the level of local culture) and coherence (achieving global significance). Thus, they have a capacity to promote a mutually intelligible discourse and *praxis* that link people across diverse settings. This can come about through Basic Christian Communities, alliances of solidarity, communication networks, scholarly organizations or, indeed, religious orders. Such processes can enable diverse contextual perspectives to cross-fertilize, strengthening local purpose and projects, while also intensifying the potential for inter-contextual learning, advocacy and small-scale economic or ecological initiatives. In such ways, new potential has been released for doing theology interculturally in a globalized world.[31] Through such interrelationships, the local can be delivered from the tendency to close in on itself through pressure of vested interests, impulses of cultural tribalism, or the despair born of disempowerment. At the same time, the global is saved from thin abstractions dis-embedded from the *matrix* of different local communities adrift from the wisdom handed on in particular traditions; no longer blind to the actual faces of suffering, no longer (in Benjamin's grim phrase) 'stepping over those who are lying prostrate.'

Thus, meaningful theological connections have been established in local-to-local and local-to-global alliances and patterns of exchange that are true to the particularity of each place, *and* open to a global horizon of life and meaning. These 'global theological flows' – however awkward-sounding the term[32] – testify to an interconnected wholeness, and, theologically, to a 'new catholicity'. More imaginatively, they suggest something of the currents, crosscurrents and undercurrents of the oceans breaking on the shores of all the continents of our one world home,[33] inviting practicable decisions on the part of Churches, ecumenical bodies – and indeed the Dominican Family – which bring people together to meet, pray, study or enter into 'covenant' with one another on matters of justice, peace and the integrity of creation.

Because of the universal impact of globalization and the emergence of new forms of systemic oppression, we need to bring to bear on the idolatry of global economic greed, ethnic violence, and ecological destruction, fresh theological thinking and symbols of a world that is mysteriously created by God, and of all humanity created in God's image; of Jesus Christ, a divine-human person who became incarnate among a particular oppressed people, who gave himself in and through his life, death and resurrection, gathering around him a localized yet eschatological community whose call was to participate in the mission of the One who had sent him to all nations and to the whole creation (Col 1:15-20). Dominicans, as members of the Church local and universal, share a common mission with the Church of Jesus Christ, whose catholicity finds expression *in and from* local Churches, in their confessing, celebrating and witnessing to the faith, hope and love of God in their midst, and at the same time part of the *missio Dei Trinitatis*, moved by the Spirit to collaborate in new forms of communion.[34] The spiritual riches of the Dominican charism are available to us, including the grace of contemplation, prayer and study, the practice of compassion with and alongside suffering people; and commitment to practical strategies for change – to release what Brueggemann has termed 'social imagination and social hope'.[35]

DOMINICANS WITNESSING IN THE GLOBAL CONTEXT

Finding new avenues for itinerant preaching and a fresh affirmation of Dominic's intention for his Order to be 'communities of sacred preaching', we need to discover small but authentic ways of building ecumenical relationships with other Churches and faiths, and of bridging between groups geographically scattered, isolated in their fragmented lifestyles, or polarized by their conflicting interests. In our own broken attempts at being community, of failing and beginning again in the ongoing journey of reconciliation and forgiveness, we can more authentically face into the pain of the world. Knowing from our daily struggles in common, the empowerment of vulnerability and the need for constant conversion, we can more humbly throw in our lot with the wider pilgrim community, encouraged to persevere in joy even as we toil, and with St Augustine, to 'sing up and keep on walking.'

Returning to the purpose and motivation of this symposium, seeking to find common source and common ground, we are aware that we come, bearing the burdens of our different histories, which however intertwined, are indeed distinct and 'other'. In this, it is necessary to avoid the tendency for Ireland to adopt the role of the en-globing Mother, or of those 'coming home' from other continents to feel constrained to vaunt their cultural independence to an extent that dialogue and encounter are foiled. Inevitably, there will be needed, all round, sensitivity as we listen, a move to harmonize conflicting interpretations of the interplay of colonialism and mission, religion and culture, or the appropriate engagement between Christianity and Primal Traditions or other World Religions.

Whatever the conflict of interpretations, we are convinced that such a symposium can open up new opportunities of mutual listening and learning, exchange of gifts, and scope for the kind of inter-cultural and counter-cultural solidarity, of which our membership of Dominican Sisters International (DSI) is already rendering practicable for us. One example of this relates to the campaign of non-violence among some Dominicans in the United Sates, who countered the jingoistic slogans of war in the name of 'homeland security', with public prayer and fasting, wearing the simple lapel badge, 'I have family in Iraq!' How incisively this cut across the dominant rhetoric which strove to domesticate all notion of international responsibility to the narrow ground of national flag, state security, or private interests.[36] Through the DSI network, these gestures of prayer and protest were taken up by Dominicans across the world. It was a case of small but courageous gesture for peace, begun in one local context, extended and amplified through a Dominican movement of 'globalization from below' demonstrating a potential for 'bridging civilizations'.

Several suggestions of solidarity are presented elsewhere in this volume, appealing to Dominican congregations who desire to read the signs of the times together, or to 'read the clouds'[37] over our changing global culture, and find new out-workings of the Dominican charism. Thus, for example, Mary O'Driscoll rightly insists that ministries of overcoming of violence or work for reconciliation belong at the core of our contemplative prayer and preaching, and call us to collaborate with others. I would wish to endorse that, and also, by way of making a final connection with the Jubilee theme and with the radical re-thinking of mission which has been going on worldwide in recent decades, point to the new global reality of uprooted peoples, as an area of mission-challenge that is centrally related to the quest for peace and reconciliation today. The call to evangelize is now recognized as germane to all our contexts, and other languages and cultures are now present close to home, as the 'other' in our midst.

Vatican II (particularly in the Decree on the Missionary Activity of the Church, *Ad Gentes*)[38] helped us towards a renewal of understanding of mission; a certain stretching of the meaning of mission beyond the limiting parameters of the previous 'go ye afar' paradigm, emerged in Paul VI's *Evangelii Nuntiandi* (1975).[39]

There is a consensus that the old paradigm of mission, like others in bygone eras, has fulfilled its potential and term.[40] Its vision and resources are inadequate to an ecological, ecumenical age. We need a more nuanced theology that keeps mission and dialogue in creative relationship, with more inflected distinctions and connections between mission, evangelization, inculturation, partnership, solidarity, power and liberation.[41] There are new raw edges to the earlier post-colonial migration of people, coupled as it is with (and often directly caused by) wars of 'ethnic cleansing', the crushing burdens of the global economy on poorer nations, with unbridled capitalism concentrating 80% of the world's resources in fewer power-blocs that are anonymous and unaccountable, and the eroding of sustainable micro- and macro-eco-systems on a global scale.[42]

This phenomenon of millions of people physically uprooted and culturally homeless, and devoid of political rights, driven from their homelands – from Rwanda, Sudan, the Congo, the Balkans, Afghanistan, East Timor, Sri Lanka and countries of the former Soviet bloc – calls for a collaborative initiative of truly catholic scope and courage. This movement of refugees, asylum-seekers and economic migrants is set to continue with an inconceivable impact, as a 'normal' feature of our global world. We (not God) have watched 'from a distance' the tragedy of exploited 'boat-people' drowning in coffin-ships, or being turned away ruthlessly from European and Australian shores, and despatched to remote detention centres without rights or recognition; whole families carried dead from haulage-carriers in the ports of Dover or Rosslare; the brutal murders of foreign women and children in Western cities, exposing what is clearly the tip of an iceberg of human trafficking and prostitution on the seamy underside of our Western cities.

A huge new challenge appears on our various horizons, which invites and encourages Dominicans to grapple towards a new vision and practice of mission that is multi-polar, and multi-directional, inter-cultural and ecumenical. To do this, missionary congregations North and South need to devise new strategies for communication, solidarity and partnership, and to share cultural experience and knowledge. They need to develop networks of support and exchange along lines indicated by Schreiter's paradigm of a 'new catholicity' and according to the new capacity made available by our resources for communication and networking. The reality of the suffering of uprooted peoples holds important implications for Dominican mission, and for testing our new-found systems of communication and inter-congregational support and partnership in ever

more strategic ways in this new century.[43] The particular focus
of this symposium with the interconnected histories of mission
– of Ireland, Portugal, the Americas, South Africa, Aotearoa-
New Zealand and Australia – with its many stories of journeys
and reverse journeys, and the daunting feats ventured to find
new ways of dialogue, evangelization, education, and of preaching the Gospel of peace, faces us squarely into the reality of a
new and different global *diaspora*. It is an issue that is worthy of
deeper reflection, prayer and conversation.

TO NEST AND TO JOURNEY –
CONTEMPLARE ET CONTEMPLATA ALIIS TRADERE
It is salutary to remember that the Irish missionary *diaspora*
of the 1860s was deeply intertwined with the Great Famine of
the 1840s. Both events have shaped Irish history in its distinct
and common themes, rooted in a shared past. Identities can
become fixated on the past, and events frozen in history. We
have had our share of that on the island of Ireland, and are once
more learning to transcend the worst aspects of 'the island
mentality', and to find causeways of reconciliation across cultures and continents. In this, we have much to learn from our
friends in such multicultural contexts as Australia and Aotearoa-
New Zealand, North America, South Africa, and Latin America,
who have struggled and suffered towards more open defini-
tions of freedom and belonging; with many standing in solidarity with those at the underside of history, those Indigenous
'others' for whom the colonial dream was a living nightmare of
dispossession, enslavement and near- genocide.

We need more generous, interdependent understandings of
identity, beyond flag and nation, transcending colour, creed
and the entrapment of any culture as an end in itself. We need
to become more practised and patient in ecumenical engagement with other Churches, faiths and traditions.

Mary Robinson, former President of Ireland, and currently

Director of the Initiative for Ethical Globalisation[44] exemplified this larger vision, more just and generous in sharing, learning not to inflict on others the pain of our own past. Speaking of emigration in terms of contribution and participation, despite its origins in sorrowful leave-taking and loss, she intimated that this great narrative has become (with some historic irony) a kind of national treasure: 'Our relationship with the *diaspora* beyond our shores is one which can instruct our society in the values of diversity, tolerance and fair-mindedness.' These words, echoing those cited by Margaret MacCurtain, stand as a symbol and a hope of what this symposium is about: 'It is like a mirror reflecting back to us on the island. It encourages us to see that Irishness is not simply territorial,'[45] but is capable of reaching out, crossing borders and oceans, embracing and being embraced by others with culture and values different from our own, who have made their own journeys and who can point to other ways of understanding that truth is diverse in its unity, compassionate in its justice, ever ancient ever new in its creative expressions.

I shall invoke one such creative expression from an Irish poet, not least because our poets were early inhabitants of this tradition of wanderers, but also because Moya Cannon's theme, 'Migrations', offers us a creative expression akin to our purpose. With its focus on 'the wild geese' (archetypal symbol of all Irish migrations, especially since the Flight of the Earls in the early seventeenth century), we receive its wisdom as a gift:

> The strong geese claim the sky again
> and tell and tell us
> of the many shifts and weathers
> of the long-boned earth.
>
> Blind to their huge, water-carved charts,
> our blood dull to the tug of poles,
> we are tuned still to the rising and dying of light

and we still share their need
to nest and to journey.[46]

Perhaps we can see in the poem an emblem for this symposium, which invites us into a long moment of recollection, into a space 'to tell and tell' our stories of 'the many shifts and weathers' we have witnessed; yet acknowledging also 'the tug of poles' and the impulse to further migration. In the ongoing sweep of our common Dominican journey, we too 'share their need / to nest and to journey', knowing the familiar double-beat of rest and of movement, of the inner and the outer call – *contemplare et contemplata aliis tradere.*

Tending the Wells of Memory – Sharing Sources of Hope

MARGARET MacCURTAIN, O.P.

When President Mary Robinson, in her inaugural speech, addressed her listeners in the historic St Patrick's Hall in Dublin Castle in 1990 she identified for millions of Irish lineage world-wide the notion of the Irish Diaspora. She spoke of a presidency that would be a symbol of what she described as the Fifth Province of Ireland.

> The Fifth Province is not anywhere here or there, north or south, east or west. It is a place within each one of us – that place which is open to the other, that swinging door, which allows us to venture out, and others to venture in … If I am a symbol of anything I would like to be a symbol of this reconciling and healing Fifth Province. [1]

This Fifth Province, she said, embraced the seventy million people of Irish descent dispersed globally. Some years later in her address, 'Cherishing the Diaspora', to the Oireachtas, the two Houses of the Irish Parliament, she expanded on the seventy million: the need to represent those invisible communities, to establish links with far-off places and countries. 'Our relations with the Diaspora beyond our shores are one which can instruct our society in the values of diversity, tolerance and fair-mindedness,' she reminded the legislators. In the course of her visits to Irish communities abroad, and during the commemoration of the Great Irish Famine in the mid-1990s she pledged to tell their stories and bring them in from the periphery to the centre. There would always be a light burning for them in the kitchen window in Áras an Uachtaráin as long as she was there.[2]

President Robinson led the Irish people to reflect on the

Great Irish Famine and to make the connection with world hunger at the end of the twentieth century. She introduced the idea, and argued it passionately, that the 1846-52 Famine defined Irish people's 'will to survive' and their sense of 'human vulnerability'. For her, commemorating the Famine was a 'moral act', a means of strengthening the bonds between present-day Ireland and its Diaspora, and of increasing good-will and concern for Third World Famine. Thus the first woman President of the Republic of Ireland released the memories of the global scattering of the Irish people over centuries, the manner in which they have inserted themselves into other cultures, how they have managed, despite lack of official recognition, to remain bonded to, while often hidden from, the homeland. Her successor, President Mary McAleese, injected new significance, other dimensions, into the achievements of the Irish Diaspora.

Born and reared in Belfast, Mary McAleese witnessed conflict and urban warfare, destruction of life and property at first-hand. Spontaneously she stretched out the hand of friendship to the unassuming communities she visited overseas since 1997. In her two visits to Australia, she addressed issues and topics that stirred her listeners' memories. Standing beside the Australian Memorial to the Irish Famine in Sydney, 13 March 2003, she dared to summon up the tragic circumstances of that catastrophe in the following words:

> The Memorial conveys to us the stark silent table on which no plate would ever again be filled, the broken families who turned their backs on it and Ireland forever, the poisoned fields they would never again till, symbolised by their abandoned spades and the eternally rotting potatoes ... From these grim things they would have to forge new hope, new lives.[2]

She movingly interpreted the panels of that remarkable piece of sculpture and singled out one representing a forgotten group:

For me, the most evocative element of the Memorial is the glass panel dividing the old life from the new, a panel which poignantly lists the names of thousands orphaned Irish girls who arrived in Sydney and found themselves within these very walls. Who can imagine what they thought and felt? Did they ever imagine that we would never forget. [3]

In an intimate aside on another occasion, she disclosed her Dominican connection at a fund-raising ball organised by the Australian Irish Society, during that second visit:

Tonight's celebration is faithful to two great characteristics, our love of company and craic and our generosity to those who are less fortunate. I am thrilled, as a Dominican girl myself, that the proceeds of this evening will go to St Lucy's Special School for the Blind, founded by the Dominican Sisters at Flatbush in 1938. It gives our gathering a depth and focus I think St. Patrick would be proud of.[4]

In tending the wells of memory and sharing sources of hope here in Tallaght associated with the Celtic saint, Aengus, and with the Dominican men and women, we are reconstructing a segment of the larger story of the Irish Diaspora, the story of the dispersal of Irish Dominican women over centuries. Identity has been described as being a dialogue with an unknown future, but its prevailing expressions are shaped by all that has gone before.[5] This essay endeavours to recall that past and weave its strands into our present consciousness. It will examine how stories are remembered, written, and – using the methodology of women's history – how stories are given fresh meanings.

Dominican women left Ireland, establishing their ministry over several centuries in purposeful ways. They were not passive victims; they possessed agency. Suellen Hoy, historian of religious women's lives, suggests that Irish women who decided to journey out became actors, responded creatively to an opportunity, and shaped their lives in a different way[6]

When that is examined, there remains the desire for a useable past in the globalized Ireland of increased affluence. Has a new sense of self, accompanying prosperity, changed our perception of an older culture? Are we capable of, willing to bestow new meanings on the history and cultural achievements of the wider Irish Diaspora with which we are familiar, and on the Dominican Diaspora which is a new concept for us? Contemporary Ireland is being shaken up and Irish identity is at the heart of the oscillations and polarizations that society is experiencing. How can we bring together the elements and tendencies that seem so wildly at variance with each other so as to constitute a whole? These questions sound abstract; but for us, too, our Dominican identity will have to be piloted into the future, successfully negotiated only if we enter into dialogue with the past of our future. Together, let us examine the significance of memory, and changing forms of expressing our sense of ourselves in the past. By weaving together various strands of that past, we will appreciate the elusive, often obscure, contribution we have made to Ireland and to the wider Diaspora.

This is our time-out to explore more awarely how nineteenth century religious communities responded to the challenges of their time, and to reclaim overlooked relationships with Dominican women of the Irish Diaspora. For those who have made the journey back, it is an opportunity to search out inherited traditions and test them in a meeting of minds and hearts.

In our shared experience of the past, sea-voyages were rites of passage. The logo designed for this Conference is of a ship, its sails billowing, its course set. The long journeys by water – to South Africa, to New Orleans, further still to Sydney Harbour in the 1860s – presented themselves to the artist and to me as the *leitmotif* of Dominican mission.[7] Even earlier than the 1860s, ocean crossings figured in the story of our foundations. The often perilous voyage across the Bay of Biscay to Portugal was the chosen route for seventeenth-century Irish women entering the only Irish convent available to them in that century of persecution, and they continued to replenish Bom Sucesso in Lisbon, strategically poised between the old world of Europe and the new across the Atlantic: the first convent of the Diaspora. In the 1850s the Lisbon convent which had survived daunting challenges to remain faithful to its founding charism, that of providing a contemplative haven for Irish women, was in serious need of reinforcement. The then prioress, Mother Theresa Staunton, applied to the flourishing Cabra community in Dublin who were in a position to respond generously. On 13 August 1860, a party of four nuns set sail for Lisbon and the following April four more Sisters arrived from Cabra. Bom Sucesso survived, its schools grew and a new chapter opened for its community.[8]

A three-decade surge in missionary activity began in the 1860s. Religious life as an adventurous calling attracted women in that period. They willingly volunteered to spread the Gospel of Christ in lands beyond Europe. The convents of Cabra, Kingstown (now Dun Laoghaire), and Sion Hill sent out some of their best members to make new foundations in South Africa, New Zealand and Australia, breathtaking enterprises for cloistered women.[9] How did those Dominican women, in their elaborate head-dresses and long sweeping habits negotiate the journey out by ship? Some kept journals and wrote long letters sent back to the home place on their arrival. Artlessly revealing, they give the flavour of the voyage and lay bare the attitudes of the writers. Such an account lies in the Dominican archives of the Maitland foundation in East Australia.

Edited and beautifully illustrated by its editor, Elizabeth Hellwig, it was in her opinion, written by Sister Hyacinth Donnellan on board the *Martha Birnie*.[10] She was one of eight chosen from their ranks by the Kingstown community for the Maitland foundation. Their leave-taking from St Mary's con-

vent and from the crowds that came to the Pier at Kingstown to
see them off on the afternoon of Saturday, 8 June 1867, was
poignantly recorded. Crossing to Plymouth, within a few days
they were on the high seas. Two months later, they experienced
a terrifying storm which the diarist recorded:

> Night came on with its accompanying rows and horrors. The
> sunset is the signal here for a squall, yet our marines will not
> admit the latter, well be it what it may. The night of Monday,
> August 5th will never be forgotten by the poor Maitlanders
> for several times we were under the water as well as over the
> water, at least so we imagined. Certainly the cannonading
> went on from 12 to 4, each splash threatening to engulf the
> "Martha". We got a partial glimpse of what was going on
> before retiring. Some would call it a grand sight, the moon
> trying to shine out from behind the clouds, waves dashing
> across the poop (for the sea was very rough) on the other
> (side) beneath and mid way between the heavens and earth
> were from 20 to 30 sailors running up the rigging like
> monkeys to reef the main sails, while some of the usual
> phrases were heard "Slack the starboard sheet", "Hold on to
> the main brace" "Let go the weather one", "Belay" ... at 4 o'c
> the wind changed again suddenly from north east to south
> west and such murder took place then! We commenced to
> say the Rosary thinking we were going down ... [11]

By the 1880s, ships crossing the Atlantic to New York, Phila-
delphia, Baltimore and New Orleans seemed as familiar to the
passengers as going by air is to travellers in the early twenty-
first century. With emigration in the 1880s rising, the ocean
routes were spectacularly busy.[12] Nora Prendiville and Alice
Nolan were two young girls bound for New Orleans who kept
diaries of their journey. Aged twenty-one and twenty respec-
tively, they went on a coaling vessel, *The Floridian*, and joined as
postulants the Dominican community in New Orleans, a foun-

dation from Cabra. Alice and Nora came from farms in the townlands of Castleisland in County Kerry and finished their schooling in Cabra boarding school outside Dublin. Determined 'to make the most and best of life' (their own words) they volunteered for religious life in New Orleans. Their diaries were written in neat black copybooks presented to them before leaving, to write for their Cabra school companions their adventures aboard ship, and to record interesting sights.[13]

They commenced their voyage at Dublin's North Wall, crossed the Irish Sea and embarked from Liverpool for the month-long journey to New Orleans. En route they travelled through the Caribbean Sea, stopping off for a day here and there at St Thomas and Port-au-Prince in the West Indies. In their round, school girls' accounts they capture the boredom of uneventful long days. Their spontaneous accounts express their unpreparedness for the world of racial diversity they encountered when *The Floridian* put in to various ports and took aboard black-skinned passengers to whom they never spoke.

Nora and Alice shared a cabin and ate at the Captain's table. Though they suffered 'seasickness, homesickness, heartsickness and any other kind of sickness you please', they recovered and learned to take a day at a time. What a contrast Nora and Alice's narrative is to an unpublished document I have in my possession. It was written by a young Irish woman who ran away from home to join the Dominican Sisters at Tacoma in Washington State on the west coast of the United States. She travelled steerage and spent her days sobbing, and writing a long, rambling apology to her mother which she posted in New York. Oblivious of her surroundings, she poured out her raw grief in page after page of incoherent love for mother and family.

Is there a literature that historicizes the Dominican Diaspora? In convent archives and among family keepsakes, there are letters and diaries, the latter requiring skilful editing if they are to be published. What other testimonies do we possess of those women who vanished into nineteenth century convents? Names on cemetery headstones? How do we remember them? How do we write them into memory?

Memories contain the map of identity. Looking at the artwork for this celebration of the shape Dominican vocation has taken in the past, we intuitively understand the relationship between text and image. Visual culture and works of the imagination speak directly to our hearts. The art of weaving a tapestry, which introduces the beholder to the themes of seascapes, the Wild Geese, the salmon of knowledge, and the cosmos discloses meanings which the confines of the written text denies.[14] Our past is woven from many threads: the golden one of narrative, the green one of exile; and if we are to pursue that image, we are reminded of the Old Irish text: 'there are three kinds of martyrdom, the red one of blood, the green one of exile, and the white one of virginity.'

Breaking silence, too often self-imposed, has produced poetry which reveals emotions about the South African mission that are more complex than historical analysis can yield. Take, for example, Maria Mackey's poem, 'The Black Madonna'.

> Soweto sprawls beneath the stars
> While Herod sleeps
> Although they're late, the hours he keeps
> In curfew'd caution;
> And, warned in dreams of other roads
> I never told him
> That I had found the Infant Christ …
> Black arms enfold Him.
> What, black? What notion?
> The dust has settled, satin-soft
> On dongas, quilted
> Above the little shoe-box house
> The Star has halted.

> I came from far, I know, a trembling stranger
> But might I not approach and touch
> That holy manger?
> O Woman! You whose lips are rich
> Whose breasts are luscious,
> Would you refuse my starving soul
> This gift so precious?
> This black-skinned bundle
> This Christ to fondle?
> She held him close, she held him fast,
> A continent in cradle,
> The cloud by day, the fire by night,
> The Truth behind the Fable,
> Before the dawn, the winds grew wild,
> The seething dust unfurled
> But, the night I came upon her
> She held the child
> She held the World
> That Black Madonna.[15]

What memories of cultural diversity, what stories of moral recognition and political resistance have our Sisters in South Africa revealed in poetry, in art, in dance and in song! Fortunately, Kathleen Boner has written the meta-narrative, the panoramic sweep of the hundred and thirty-five years since six young Irish Dominican women embarked on the sailing vessel, *The Saxon*, bound for the Cape of Good Hope. In the words of Marian O'Sullivan who as vicar of the Region of South Africa gave courageous leadership during the critical years of apartheid:[16]

Since the first foundation of the Irish Dominicans in Cape Town hundreds of young Irish women have left their homes in order to minister to the people in this beautiful and challenging country. Some returned home enriched, having given the best years of their lives to the mission. Most stayed and were joined by South Africans, and all of these through their educational apostolate, contributed to the growth of the church in the sub-continent.[16]

It is a powerful story of personal experience and empathy with other cultures. The strength of Kathleen Boner's history is its spirited authenticity based on original documentary sources, oral testimonies, and rigorous scholarship. *A Time To Speak* is a definitive volume on the life and work of the Irish Dominican Sisters in South Africa. Perusing the Introduction, the reader is struck by the number of specialised studies published in the 1990s: Rose O'Neill's *A Rich Inheritance: Galway Dominican Nuns, 1644—* (Dominican Sisters, Galway, 1994); Sr Nicholas Griffey's first-person account of the pedagogy of the deaf in Ireland, *From Silence to Speech* (Dominican Publications, Dublin, 1994); several other narratives of Dominican presence in South Africa; Mary O'Driscoll's *Catherine of Siena* (Editions du Signe, Strasbourg, 1994).

The motif of weaving to which we have returned in this gathering found its voice in an enlightening anthology, edited by Dominique Horgan, *Weavings: Celebrating Dominican Women* (Dublin, 1988). Mary O'Byrne takes up the theme of weaving in her lively account of the presence of Irish Dominican Sisters in South America from 1968 onwards. Her book, *Strands from a Tapestry* (Dominican Publications, Dublin, 2001) speaks to the reader in the language of liberation.

Research is solitary work, sometimes lonely. Flowing into the publications are the theses accepted readily at graduate and post-graduate levels in universities world wide. It was not always so! Thirty years ago there was no question of doing research in women's history. In my own situation I was admonished by two scholarly professors in different universities that I would be well advised to study the life of a bishop for my post-graduate degree. The writing of Dominican women's history has moved spectacularly into the category of professional history, passing from the stage of recovering information to one of constructing women as historical subjects, no longer relegated to footnotes, or treated as auxiliaries to churchmen.

The second stage goes beyond the simple search for roots; it is concerned with recognising religious women's agency in their time, setting them in the context of their age. To achieve this objective is to question the accepted chronology, and at times to challenge the accepted version of what happened. Kathleen Boner accomplishes that. So did Assumpta O'Hanlon in her study of the status controversy: were 'active' Dominicans second or third Order of Preachers?, a nineteenth-century legacy of dispute. (*Dominican Pioneers in New South Wales*, Australasian Publishing Co., Sydney, 1949). Sometimes to name an issue is to clear the air. Disclosure is a challenge to the professional historian; for it is only by disclosure, revealing the facts, however uncomfortable they may be, that hierarchy crumbles.

That being said, much professional history avoids transparency, pleading insufficient knowledge of the context of the situation. What is context? What does contextualising the event mean? It has to do with establishing chronology and with placing women's activities in a meaningful setting. We learned a set of dates in school history, selected as a kind of unchangeable canon – for example, 1798 and the United Irishmen; the Great Irish Famine 1846-52; Parnell and Home Rule 1886; the 1916 Rebellion. Historians of women's history have only recently examined the validity of that established chronology. If women are acknowledged as agents of important events, then their dates should enter the canon, as it is termed. A significant date for women's history, and for the social history of Ireland, was the Dublin foundation in 1815 of the Sisters of Charity who worked among the poor of the city and in the course of their ministry demonstrated how to engage, humanely and competently, in practical social work.

In Diaspora history, Suellen Hoy has designated First Wave and Second Wave religious women emigrants to the United States in the nineteenth century.[17] The pioneering generation of the First Wave were founders who were invited by bishops and influential priests, most often Irish by birth, into their dioceses and parishes abroad. Resourceful, authoritative women, they possessed leadership qualities and worked with the clergy. Builders of convents, schools and hospitals, they had vision and were not afraid to take risks. Mother Gabriel Gill who led a group of ten Sisters from Sion Hill convent in Blackrock in 1870 to establish the Dominicans in the new diocese of Otago in New Zealand, supervised five more foundations in South Island before setting out for Western Australia in her sixties to make a foundation. Less colourful but equally intrepid, Mother Columba Boylan in Maitland, Mother Dympna Kinsella in Capetown, and Mother Rose Whitty in Port Elizabeth, South Africa, established enduring foundations.[18]

They, in turn, recruited younger, less forceful women who consolidated the missions. Second Wave religious women went into the schools. They became administrators who dealt more formally with their clergy and with city councils. All came back to Ireland to recruit. In the thirty-five years, 1875-1910, the Cabra Dublin community sent out another twenty professed Sisters, two novices and two postulants. Suellen Hoy closes her analysis of Second Wave religious women as the great transatlantic migrations to the United States tailed off with the onset of World War One. For Australia, World War Two and the 1950s marked the end of recruitment from Ireland. South Africa continued to be supported by Irish women who volunteered for the South African enterprise during the years of apartheid. Those were the years when the Kerdiffstown novitiate in Ireland sent numbers of Dominican Sisters to South Africa. For Lisbon and New Orleans support continues to the present.

Diaspora history is well contextualized, but it is rare for

posterity not to soften and smooth away the rough, the raw, and the discordant which were the sources of creative energy. Our Dominican Diaspora has experienced apartheid and the ending of it; segregation of black America and desegregation; the divisiveness of class within religious communities and the abolition of status and hierarchy after the Second Vatican Council. We have all moved from an inward-looking and insulated life-style to one that challenges as well as invites us to grow in self-actualization. We have transformed roles in the Church which our founding Sisters would never have wished us to perpetuate, into ministries that give us scope to act autonomously and as individuals. In the last thirty years we have changed our mission in ways that would have startled but not surprised, our nineteenth-century forerunners.

Which of us does not respond to the courage of Áine Hardiman and Feargal Cassidy, arrested 28 August 1985 (and later imprisoned) during the march to Pollsmoor prison to deliver a letter to Nelson Mandela? Four Dominican Sisters – Áine Hardiman, Sheila Mullan, Feargal Cassidy and Caitriona Owens – took part in the march, joining teachers and students in a massed, silent protest of over a thousand people. Áine Hardiman's account of the event is a corroboration of what Martin Luther King called the 'unstoppability' of the civil and human rights movements of the second half of the twentieth century.

The loud hailer ordered us to disperse. We stood. The command to charge was given and people started running helter skelter with police in hot pursuit brandishing shambuks, quirts, batons. The teacher beside me said: Sister, just stand … One man as he passed us raised his baton and brought it down on the head of my companion. Patrick lost his balance and fell. I bent down to help him and the TV crews were on top of us. A TV man asked him if he was alright. I shall never forget the dignity and strength of Patrick's answer 'I'm OK and I want to tell you this. We *shall* overcome'. [19]

It gets worse The protestors regrouped and Áine and Feargal were invited to march with the clergy at the front of the 2000-strong column of marchers, resolute witnesses to the spiritual values of the movement. Sr Áine continues:

> We linked arms and silently wended our way round the side streets that led to Kroomboom Road. The caspirs etc. were there ahead of us, about 500m. The silence deepened as we walked towards the massed array of force. We clung to one another more tightly as we advanced and prayed softly. It was for me a moment of vision what the new S.A. could be – all races, all creeds, and none, walking arm in arm into danger for justice.

This is story at its climax. 'The true story exists in the taking up of the counter-thread of the time. The history of this moving into counter-direction is exactly the Golden Thread of the Dominican Family story, the thread woven into the more serene whole'. Words uttered by Fr Edward Schillebeeckx in a memorable lecture he delivered in 1983, *The Golden Thread*.[20] 'Without a story we would be void of remembrances of the past,' he reminded his listeners; and he implied that by critical reflection on the story we discern new possibilities for action. 'I live by my own story,' Schillebeeckx said simply. 'When I became a Dominican I tied the narrative of my life to the one of the Dominican Family'. However, he warned: 'if we just repeat the story in a sterile, unimaginative way we lose the Golden Thread'.

Schillebeeckx identifies a vibrant spirituality as the means of testing the quality of our particular narrative. The story of Dominic as founder, and that of Jesus as model are the core narratives which shape our Dominican identity. Dominican women have the further enrichment of our founding histories that balance out the paternal narrative. To state that is to acknowledge that retrieving our own story as Dominican *women*, publishing and reading it, pondering on it and sharing insights about our commonalities is to recognise that our counter-thread is woven into the Golden Thread.

Can a case be made for nostalgia, for recalling past times, or are those who left Ireland better off for forgetting Ireland? Nostalgia has an element of loss in recollecting a static past, a 'things will never be the same' refrain which saps the energy. Nostalgia breeds pessimism at its most seductive; and hope is the barometer that reads whether we are on a nostalgic trip, or actually drawing sustenance from the sources of our identity. Emily Dickinson, poet of spiritual considerations, likens hope to a thing with feathers 'that perches in the soul', and sings without words even in the harshest gales, in 'the chillest land', and 'on the strangest sea', undemanding, constant,

> Yet, never, in Extremity,
> It asked a crumb – of me. [21]

We have to ask ourselves whether the notion of an Irish 'spiritual empire' is a misconception, a spiritual alternative to the material power of the British Empire in the nineteenth century? Instead of perpetuating the cliché that Irish religious women followed the flag of empire and traded on it for their identity, let us state firmly, on the evidence of our past record, that we followed our people into exile and emigration, that we ministered to them, that we spread the Gospel of Christ, providing education and stability. When the demand for civil rights arose in the 1960s we connected with the larger movement for racial justice and the struggle for reconciliation as well as for peace. That is the real story of our Dominican Diaspora.

President Mary Robinson has been credited with re-imagining the Irish Diaspora, and Irish people, particularly those under sixty, understood her language. She made the connection between the Great Irish Famine, world hunger and human rights. In the 1990s the Irish became one of the most globalized people on the planet and were ready to explore issues of assimilation and identity in a multi-cultural context. Images of the Diaspora changed, and Irish society finally was reconciled with the memories of the Great Famine and became receptive to more positive evaluations of their global contribution. How has Ireland shaped the character of the peoples that Irish immigrants settled among? How can the descendants of those immigrants in Australia, New Zealand, South Africa, and the United States help the Irish, with their new and still fragile sense of self-sufficiency, to appreciate diversity and to close the gap of social and economic inequalities?

In reflecting on what I have named our Dominican Diaspora, we add to that larger discourse our experience of bringing all sections of society together in processes of reconciliation and development, not just overseas, but in Ireland, north and south. Our conversation will, inevitably, dwell on contemporary concerns while reaching back through our history to evaluate the prism of choices our ancestors possessed and how well they chose. This time is our Fifth Province, a space set aside by the thoughtful planners of this gathering to allow us all to be at home to each other, to claim our common identity, and dare to set sail again into the future.

In Praise of Valiant Women: Women and the Word

ANNE THURSTON

Let us now sing the praises of famous women,
our foremothers in their generations.
The Lord apportioned to them great glory,
his majesty from the beginning.
There were those who ruled in
their realms,
and made a name for themselves
by their valour;
those who gave counsel because
they were intelligent;
those who spoke in prophetic oracles;
those who led people by their counsels
and by their knowledge of a people's lore;
they were wise in the words of their instruction;
those who composed musical tunes
or put verses in writing.

You will recognise these verses from Sirach 44:1-5, and their
transposition into a new key! Elisabeth Schüssler Fiorenza in a
recent work talks about the effect on women of grammatically
androcentric language in scripture: 'wo/men always have to
think twice and deliberate whether we are meant or not … '[1]
When does 'men' mean 'men and women', when 'men only'?

Well in this case 'famous men' meant famous men, and
clearly not women, as Sirach continues in six further chapters
and one hundred and eighty verses to name and praise male
rulers, teachers, leaders, and prophets. In Ireland, on November 6, we celebrate the feast of All Saints of Ireland, and Sirach
44.1-15 is read in all its exclusive glory; and all around the

country the majority of women who make up the congregations listen as they are erased from the history of the holy ones. The wise or awake among them murmur 'not counting women', and Saint Brigid looks down ruefully.

Sirach recognises that some worthy of praise have been forgotten, 'But of others there is no memory; they have perished as though they had never existed; become as though they had never been born' (Sir 44:9). Although, once again, he is referring to men, this has been the fate of most women.

In many cases the names have been lost and we are left with the tantalising 'Anon' which has become in many cases women's thumbprint. Poet Carol Ann Duffy has penned a witty piece about this phenomenon, and I am citing the first and last verse from her poem of that title:

> If she were here
> she'd forget who she was,
> it's been so long,
> maybe a nurse, a nanny,
> maybe a nun –
> Anon.

> But I know best –
> how she passed on her pen
> like a baton
> down through the years,
> with a hey nonny
> hey nonny
> hey nonny no –
> Anon.[2]

On a more serious and hopeful note we might look to another source in our scriptures and remember the promise from the Book of Wisdom:

Although she is but one, she can do all things,

and while remaining in herself, she renews all things;
in every generation she passes into
holy souls,
and makes them friends of God,
and prophets (Wis 7:27).

This event is an occasion to celebrate the friends of God and prophets in the Dominican Order and among its associates. However, we are also interested in recalling the foremothers of our faith in our tradition and in our scriptures. There is a need, in the first place, to lament the erasure of women and their silencing in our faith tradition and then, as a second phase, to engage in the work of retrieval and remembrance so that we recognise that we do indeed have strong threads connecting us back to the originating story of our faith – and not just through its fathers, but through its mothers and grandmothers. Then, finally, we could celebrate these women and write their names, not in the book of Sirach where we would need to 'add and stir', but in the continuing book of Sophia where there is already space: 'in every generation she passes into holy souls'.

The shape of this discourse – lament, memory, and hope or celebration – is now a commonly practised one among feminist scholars, perhaps best known in terms of the method of hermeneutics developed by Elisabeth Schüssler Fiorenza and adopted by many other scholars: a Hermeneutics of Suspicion, Retrieval, Proclamation and Creative Imagination. In a recent work Fiorenza talks about learning the dance steps of wisdom's ways of interpretation with its commitment to liberation and justice.[3]

I have chosen to focus on two significant women leaders, one from the Hebrew scriptures and one from the New Testament. Both women stand at powerful transformative moments in the faith history. Neither woman, unusually, is described either as wife or mother; both women have been subject to a distortion of their stories and their memories; both are susceptible to the process of discerning their story through lament, retrieval and celebration. And, finally, although you will know these stories very well – too well, maybe – I remain confident that we can retrieve them in ways which will encourage us, enliven our discourse, give us hope and cause for celebration, sending us to call out in the streets, 'Come eat of my bread, drink of the wine I have mixed' (Prov 9:5).

My chosen valiant women of the Word are Miriam the prophet and Mary of Magdala, the apostle. And, of course, the latter whose feast we celebrated recently is of particular importance to Dominican women as she is the patron of their Order.

MIRIAM

No one who writes about Miriam now can ignore the debt to Phyllis Trible one of the first feminist scholars to bring her 'Out of the Shadows'.[4] As Trible points out, the call for justice now requires that we listen for the voice of Miriam rather than the familiar voice of Moses. We all know about the baby in the bulrushes, the theophany on Mount Sinai, the tablets of stone; we need to listen more attentively to catch the strains of Miriam's song. How appropriate to the theme of this conference, 'From Threads to Tapestry', that we pick up the different threads of Miriam's story and weave the bits and pieces, scattered as they are, into a new pattern.

I want to retell her story, evoking the symbols of water and wilderness as her domain. She may enter the story without name or lineage: 'his sister', we are told, 'stood at a distance' (Ex 2:4), as women do. But we notice that this woman stands at the service of life and not to watch death by drowning. This water will be living water: just as the breaking of waters had signalled birth, so this placing on the waters will bring new life. And Miriam's 'watching' quickly changes to the role of mediator and leader: 'Shall I go and call a nurse?' So the girl went and called. (Ex 2:7,8). Miriam and her mother act to subvert the power of the Pharaohs and in so doing they work with the same wit and wisdom as the Hebrew midwives Shiphrah and Puah who saved the lives of the male children (Ex 1:15). In fact, the saving of the child involves a community of women: the mother, the sister, the daughter of the Pharaoh. We have become too familiar with the sickening sanitised phrase 'collateral damage' to explain the deaths of civilians in war; here we have its opposite – collaboration for the sake of life and between sworn enemies. In 1923, a woman economist reflected on the differences, as she saw them, between death-based and birth-based religions. For the birth-based religion, the main question is not 'What is going to happen after I die?'– from which the cult of the suicide martyrs arises – but 'What is to be done for the child who is born?'[5] In our time, essayist Barbara Kingsolver suggests that those who make decisions to drop bombs should first 'spend a whole day taking care of a baby. 'We were not meant to do this killing thing.' she insists.[6]

'Sister of Moses', we answer, when asked who Miriam is. Let us rename her here in her own right as Life-Giver, Life-Sustainer, as Woman of Wit, as Daughter of Wisdom. Her place in our book is already assured and her story has only just begun.

Miriam disappears from the story and attention shifts to Moses. Remember we have not yet heard her name.

When she emerges again, Miriam has a name, a role and a title and so surprising is this insertion that we should quote it in full:

> Then the prophet Miriam, Aaron's sister, took a tambourine in her hand; and all the women went out after her with tambourines and with dancing. And Miriam sang to them:
> 'Sing to the Lord, for he has triumphed gloriously;
> horse and rider he has thrown into the sea.'(Ex 15:20,21)

Miriam the prophet! This is her title; this is her designation. But the words of her song sound somewhat familiar. These are the opening lines of the song ascribed to Moses, giving thanks for the parting of the seas. Phyllis Trible[7] – supported by other scholars – argues that the song should be attributed to Miriam and that later redactors ascribed it to Moses. It is a comment on the tenacity of the Miriamic tradition that the remnant survives. 'You've taken the words right out of my mouth,' we say; and they did, and they continue to do so. 'Hey nonny nonny no'!

But as we pick up the thread of Miriam's story, which started by the waters and continues there, we find her once more in the company of women and once again leading them – 'and all the women went out after her' – and we begin to understand what Elisabeth Fiorenza means about reading with a hermeneutics of suspicion. In whose interest was that tradition suppressed? But at the same time, we begin to delight in joining the steps of wisdom's dance and, like the women, following Miriam's music.

And as we conclude the second chapter of her story, how shall we name 'the sister of Aaron' now? Miriam the prophet, Miriam the Leader of Women, Miriam the Musician.

We pick up the threads again in the Book of Numbers where a dark shadow is cast over our heroine, although in the circumstances that image is perhaps not the right one, as we shall see. Chapter 12 opens with Miriam and Aaron speaking out against Moses because he has married a Cushite woman.

Whatever about the reasons for criticising Moses, it is the following lines which strike a chord with us: 'Has the Lord spoken only through Moses? Has he not spoken through us also?' (Num 12:2). Miriam's understanding of leadership and authority, as we have seen from the beginning of her story, is an authority exercised in community.

But the Lord is displeased, and summons the three of them to the tent of meeting where his anger is kindled against Miriam and Aaron and he affirms the position of Moses. When the cloud has departed Miriam's face is transfigured and 'she has become leprous, as white as snow' (Num12:10). This is a precise reversal of the situation when Moses entered the tent of meeting and emerged with the 'skin of his face shining' (Ex 34:35). Miriam is singled out for punishment, suggesting that it is she rather than Aaron who threatens the authority. Though Aaron and Moses plead for their sister, she is shut out from the camp for seven days.

But that is not the end of the story, for we learn that 'the people did not set out on the march until Miriam had been brought in again' (Num 12:15). The God of Moses may have turned against her but the people remain faithful to their leader.

This conflict, settled in such a harsh way by the crushing of the voice of Miriam, is not the only memory carried in the tradition. There is another thread which we may weave into our tapestry. In the book of Micah there is a lament, now known to us through the Good Friday Reproaches:

> O my people what have I done to you?
> In what have I wearied you?
> Answer me!
> For I brought you up from the land of Egypt
> and redeemed you from the house of slavery.

But missing from that liturgy are the following lines:

> And I sent before you Moses,
> Aaron and Miriam (Mic 6:3,4).

The prophetic tradition carries that memory of the three prophets, Moses, Aaron *and* Miriam, and once again the cultic or priestly tradition suppresses it. However, the red thread which links these references to Miriam suggests that this is a voice not easily silenced and, furthermore, that leadership was exercised by all three.

With the people patiently waiting for Miriam's return we might sing the lament for her: 'O my God what have I done to you? How have I offended you?'

Indeed, her offence and her punishment will continue to serve as a warning for future generations: 'Remember what the Lord your God did to Miriam on your journey out of Egypt' (Deut 24.9). This in contrast to Aaron who was not punished and indeed whose name is exalted in the Book of Sirach: 'a holy man like Moses'; and the praise continues for sixteen verses (Sir 45:6-22).

How shall we name her now, this sister of Moses and Aaron? Miriam the Suffering One, Miriam the Brave, Miriam Rejected but not Abandoned by Her People?

The time of her birth was not noted in the annals, but her death is. When the whole congregation comes into the wilderness we are told that Miriam died there and was buried there. Even then her death becomes a cause of impurity as the law had just been given which stated that anyone coming into contact with a dead body would be unclean for seven days (Num 19:14). Thus the last memory of Miriam is that of contamination, immediately followed by the line, 'Now there was no water for the congregation' (Num 20:2). It is as if when Miriam dies the very source of life dries up. According to Phyllis Trible, 'Nature mourns her demise.' [8]

In trying to restore this woman to our memory we can see a struggle in the tradition to accommodate her between priestly and prophetic strands. But perhaps of even greater significance is the memory of Miriam as leader of song and dance, a liturgical leader of her people: 'Then the prophet Miriam took a tambourine in her hand; and all the women went out after her with tambourines and with dancing. And Miriam sang to them … ' (Ex 15:20). Not only is she forgotten on Good Friday but also at the Easter Vigil when her song is given to Moses who by his own admission was a poor speaker (Ex 6:28)!

Do we, as Trible suggests, catch echoes of the songs of Miriam in lines in the psalms 'Raise a song and sound the tambourine' (Ps 81:2) and 'the girls playing tambourines' (Ps 68:25)? Our iconography abounds with images of David and his harp. But should it not equally abound with images of Miriam and her tambourine? Of course these songs of the women can be songs of joy and triumph; but they are also songs of lament. We think of Jepthah's daughter who came out to meet her father with timbrels and dancing and of how her song was turned to mourning, and there arose a custom thereafter that the daughters of Israel would go out to lament the daughter of Jephtah (Judg 11:40). Did the daughters of Israel also lament the death of their leader and prophet Miriam?

But the voice of Miriam as prophetic singer of her people's liberation is far from lost to the tradition when we recall another Miriam, Miriam of Nazareth, who sings out her *Magnificat* of praise at the beginning of the Gospel of Luke. There is another tantalising little connection between Luke's women, whose encounter issues, not just in the births of their sons, but also of their songs, and the women of Exodus. If Mary bears the Hebrew name Miriam, as did the sister of Aaron (Ex 15:20); Elizabeth bears the Hebrew name Elisheba as did the wife of Aaron (Ex 6:23).[9] 'The Lord is my strength and my might,' sang Miriam of Exodus; 'The Lord has shown strength with his arm,' sings Miriam of Nazareth. And the song in the hill town, in the house which has become the house of women, with the door of the temple and the mouth of the priest Zechariah closed, catches up another song, that of the once barren Hannah: 'My heart exults in the Lord, my strength is exalted in my God' (1 Sam 2:1).

The singing of Miriam has not been stilled and rings out whenever women gather to lift their voices in praise and join that company of valiant women passing the baton down from Miriam to the great medieval Abbess Hildegard of Bingen. 'There were those who composed musical tunes or put their verses into writing'(Sir 44:5). And we write their names, these valiant women, into the Book of Wisdom.

MARY MAGDALENE

'Does the Lord speak only through Moses?' asked Miriam; 'Does the Lord speak only through Peter?' Mary Magdalene might well have asked. In an article in *The Tablet* at Easter 1998, theologian Gerald O'Collins argued the case for the primacy of Peter's witness. 'It may well be that Mary Magdalene was the first chronologically to see Jesus gloriously risen from the dead … But … it is Peter who leads a group of witnesses to the resurrection.' And, later, '*After* Mary Magdalene, Simon Peter was the first to whom the risen Lord disclosed himself.'[10] (Italics mine.) Feminist scripture scholar Sandra Schneiders comments, not on this article, but on this tendency: 'Until quite recently postpatristic commentators have, virtually to a man (and I use the word designedly), treated the appearance to Mary Magdalene as a minor, private, personal, or unofficial encounter between Jesus and his (hysterical?) female follower, in which he kindly consoles her before making his official and public Easter appearances to male witnesses and commissioning them to carry on his mission to the world.'[11]

Note, though, the reference to *post*patristic commentators; for in the first centuries of the Church no writer misinterpreted Mary Magdalene as a prostitute.[12] It was Hippolytus of Rome (*ca* 170 – *ca* 235) who first acknowledged her as 'Apostle to the Apostles' and linked Mary Magdalene with the Bride of the Canticles, and this is still reflected in the lectionary reading for her feastday. She was the most popular female saint of the Middle Ages, and from the thirteenth century to the fifteenth her feast ranked as one of the great feasts of the year[13] (subsequently reduced to a memorial). 'No other woman in the world was shown greater reverence or believed to have greater glory in heaven,' wrote a thirteenth century vicar-general of the Dominican order.[14] There was a widespread cult of Mary Magdalene in medieval France with various churches laying claim to her relics.[15] I asked my Dominican friends whether

Mary Magdalene had been chosen as patron of their Order because she was seen as a suitable model for an order of preachers as the first preacher of the resurrection, or because she was seen as a model of penitence for an order preaching repentance. Although both reasons are given it appears that the penitent sinner was irresistible, particularly for male preachers dwelling on sexual sin and, of course, making the now popularised connection between Mary Magdalene and the 'woman in the city who was a sinner' in Luke 7. This identification was first made by Pope Gregory I, and has proved to be the most difficult association to break. Yet, there were counter-voices also in the medieval period, most notably Christine de Pisan (1364-1430) who wrote in her *Book of the City of Ladies*:

> If women's language had been so blameworthy and of such small authority, as some men argue, our Lord Jesus Christ would never have deigned to wish so worthy a mystery as His most gracious resurrection to be first announced by a woman, just as he commanded the blessed Magdalene.[16]

However, it was Mary Magdalene's association with the prostitute which was to cling to her until corrected by relatively recent scholarship. Starting with the order of the penitents of St Mary Magdalene in 1227, down to the notorious Magdalene Asylums which existed in many countries, including Ireland, from 1765 to 1992,[17] and supported by art and literature, the image of the long-haired and weeping Magdalene, rather than the witness of the resurrection, is the one which has endured. This is perhaps not surprising as there are still women witnesses to the cruelty and shame of life in the Magdalene laundries.[18] The juxtaposition between the Blessed Virgin and the repentant sinner fired the imagination of preachers. The following example comes from a popular nineteenth century Dominican preacher:

> The woman breathing purity, innocence, grace, receives the

Congregation of Dominican Sisters, Cabra, Ireland

This tapestry features the cosmos still in the process of creation;
contrasting textures and colours bring to life both natural landscape
and animal husbandry; the salmon of wisdom caught on a golden
line, rises towards the Trinity knot intimating the Congregation's
education ministry, and the shield-like discs the motto – *Laudare,*
Benedicere, Praedicare; the Atlantic Wild Geese are emblematic of
our missionaries who journeyed to the very distant lands represented
at the symposium

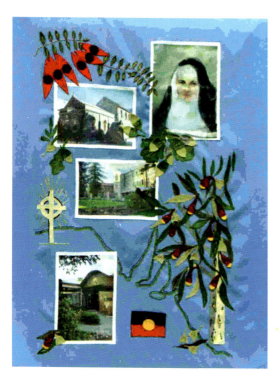

Congregation of the Holy Cross, Cabra, South Australia

This banner portrays their Foundress Mother M. Teresa Moore; and significant places of the sisters' ministry, with symbols of their Irish heritage and their deep roots in the Australian landscape against a background of Pacific blue.

Dominican Sisters of Western Australia

The Aboriginal 'Message Stick', points to the different sites of the sisters' ministry – bringing the gospel message to rural outback, gold mining towns and inner-city communities.

woman whose breath is the pestilence of hell! Extremes meet. Mary the Virgin takes the hand of Mary the Magdalene; and, in the organised charity of the Church of God, the penitent enters in to be saved and sanctified.[19]

I have painted a picture in broad strokes in order to suggest some of the presuppositions we may bring to our reading of the scriptures in relation to Mary Magdalene. The waters are muddied to quite a remarkable degree in relation to this woman. In fact there is perhaps no other figure apart from Mary, mother of Jesus, whose myth and popular understanding so outstrip scriptural evidence. It is also clear that the myth and history of Mary Magdalene in the tradition bring a legacy of both pain and promise for women. There are so many layers overlaying the biblical picture that it is almost impossible to retrieve the woman disciple, follower of Jesus, as Luke tells us (8:2). Our task is to return to those scriptures and see if we can reclaim Mary of Magdala as a valiant woman of the Word, inspiring the mission and ministry of Dominican women in particular, but also of all women who feel themselves commissioned to 'Go, tell!'

Let us begin, though, with that brief reference in Luke's Gospel:

> Soon afterwards he went on through cities and villages, proclaiming and bringing the good news of the kingdom of God. The twelve were with him as well as some women who had been cured of evil spirits and infirmities: Mary called Magdalene from whom seven demons had gone out … (Lk 8:1,2).

Part of the work of retrieval of Mary Magdalene has, rather fittingly, been carried out by two Dominican women scholars: Barbara Reid, O.P. and Mary Catherine Hilkert, O.P.[20] Barbara Reid states quite categorically, 'The idea that she [Mary Magdalene] was a prostitute has no basis in the New Testament.

Nor is there any indication that she was a sinner.'[21] Indeed Reid offers a challenging interpretation of the story of the woman 'who was a sinner', questioning our assumptions about her, while continuing to insist that she is not linked with Mary Magdalene. She quickly dismisses suggestions that the seven demons indicate sinfulness, reminding us that many illnesses were attributed to demonic possession.

So, applying a hermeneutics of suspicion to the tradition linking the texts, we might ask: In whose interest was this connection made? Abandoning conspiracy theories, let us describe it as, at best misguided and confused; at worst, a reflection of women assuming that 'most women (insofar as they are interesting at all) are whores and Jesus' paradigmatic relationship with women is centered on saving them from sexual sins.'[22]

A hermeneutic of retrieval reveals a very simple explanation: Mary Magdalene had been ill and now was healed. Reid reminds us of the symbolic significance of the number seven signifying wholeness. Unfortunately, in the Gospel of Luke she belongs to that group of Galilean women who are not believed and not commissioned. The legacy of Luke in dismissing the witness of women as 'an idle tale' has continued in one form or another to this day. And this despite the fact that the other three Gospels carry accounts of commissioning the Galilean women – Mark 16:7; Matthew 28:7; 10, and John 20:17. In all four accounts one name is constant, that of Mary Magdalene. It seems quite clear that she is a recognised leader among the women disciples and is usually found in the company of other women. John, as is typical in that Gospel, deals with her separately.

However before we come to that account, it is worth observing at this point the importance of the other women. As with Miriam, this woman should not be isolated from her community. It is a point to which I will return later.

Does the short text from Luke 8 offer any challenge to contemporary women? Barbara Reid reflects on women today who put their resources at the disposal of the Church, 'sometimes questioning whether they are being co-opted into perpetuating a structure in which they can never have access to presbyteral ministry and decision-making power. Like the Galilean women they continue to make it possible for the men to assume all the public ministries and leadership positions.'[23] While we might query 'never', the point is well made. Would a revised image of Mary Magdalene see her as one supporting Church order, or challenging it? Does she fit our image of priest or prophet? At the very least, at the end of this section from Luke, we can note that she was a disciple and part of the preaching mission of Jesus.[24]

So, picking up the thread from our renaming of Miriam, we might ask about how we might name Mary Magdalene now? No longer the reformed prostitute, no longer the woman who wept and washed the feet of Jesus, though blessed be her memory too. No longer the sister of Martha, Mary the contemplative, Mary of Bethany, however praiseworthy her calling. This Mary Magdalene, healed of her illness, can be recalled here as follower, as disciple, as one who ministered (*diakonein*), as preacher of the good news.

As we turn now to the Gospel of John we come to the fullest portrait of this woman. John situates her first at the foot of the cross together with the mother of Jesus (never named in this Gospel) and her sister, Mary, the wife of Clopas. The disciple whom Jesus loved is also there (Jn19:25,26). Many Western artists have depicted this scene, as well as the scene in the garden, but at the cross Mary Magdalene is always distinguished from the mother of Jesus by her long flowing hair and often by her weeping at the feet.[25]

The resurrection narrative circles round two questions which have haunted women ever since, 'Woman, why are you weeping? Whom are you seeking?' These questions remain pertinent as women today weep for the loss of all that has been denied them and yet continue to seek the Christ: 'Tell me where you have laid him.'

The story opens: 'Early on the first day of the week while it was still dark, Mary Magdalene came to the tomb and saw that the stone had been removed from the tomb.'(Jn 20:1). It is 'still dark', we hear, and we remember John's Gospel with its rich symbolism of dark and light, and we know that what one can see in the dark is limited. We see that there is a journey to be made which begins with 'running' and ends with 'telling', but which will have a still centre of 'knowing'. The journey begins with anxiety ('We do not know where they have laid him', Jn 20:2), continues with distress and lamentation ('as she wept'), and then turns round to recognition ('Rabbouni').

It is a journey of transformation not dissimilar to that made by the disciples on the road to Emmaus, a journey from *blindness* – 'Jesus came near but their eyes were kept from recognising him' (Lk 24:15); 'she saw Jesus standing there but did not know that it was he' (Jn 20:14) – to *sight* – 'their eyes were opened'(Lk 24:31); 'She turned and said to him in Hebrew "Rabbouni!" ...' (Jn 20:16) – to *insight* – 'and he vanished from their sight ... that same hour they got up' (Lk 24:31,33); 'Do not hold on to me ... but go and say ... Mary Magdalene went and announced to the disciples, "I have seen the Lord" ... '(Jn 20:17,18).

Sandra Schneiders also divides the episode into three sections: blindness; turning; announcing.[26] Schneiders draws our attention to the connection between the search for the beloved in the Song of Songs and this Easter garden, a link, recognised in the Roman Missal and the First Reading for the memorial; and of course it also evokes the garden of the creation account. However, there is another resonance, that with the garden where Jesus is arrested. Although John does not have a scene of agony in the garden, he does have a dramatic dialogue of betrayal which also centres round the identity of Jesus. 'Whom are you looking for?' (Jn 18:4), Jesus asks of Judas and the soldiers. 'Jesus of Nazareth,' they answer. 'I am he,' replies Jesus, and again asks, 'Whom are you looking for?' and three times the response 'I am he' is repeated (Jn18:5,6,8).

Judas and his soldiers seek to take Jesus alive and lead him to his death; Mary Magdalene seeks a dead body but finds the living Christ. This kind of seeking of Jesus has marked the Gospel of John from the beginning and has characterised the true disciple. 'What are you looking for?' Jesus asks the disciples of John (Jn1:35), and the invitation which follows is, 'Come and see' (Jn 1:39,46). This gentle invitation, taken up and issued in her turn by the Samaritan woman to her townspeople (Jn 4:29), is in sharp contrast to the taking and binding of Jesus by the soldiers in the garden (Jn 18:12).

Before Mary can respond to 'Whom are you looking for?' she has to overcome her sorrow: 'Why are you weeping?' She is asked the question twice: first by the angels, and then by Jesus, whom she supposes to be the gardener. As Sandra Schneiders points out, there is a 'delicious irony' in Mary's essentially correct identification of Jesus.[27] However, as she is preoccupied with her search for a missing body – 'Tell me where you have laid him and I will take him away' (Jn 20:15) – she fails to recognise that it is indeed Jesus, a living person. But her lamentation and bitter weeping will lead her through the darkness and across the threshold into the light of the resurrection. Catherine Hilkert describes this moment of breakthrough:

> Her greatest hope had been to find the dead body of the one she loved. Instead that hope was broken open beyond all expectation, and she experienced the mystery and power of the resurrection in the calling of her name.[28]

This epiphany comprises a single verse which Sandra Schneiders describes as one of the most moving in the New

Testament.[29]

> Jesus said to her, 'Mary!' She turned and said to him in
> Hebrew, 'Rabbouni!' (which means Teacher) (Jn 20:16).

The joy of recognition, being called by her name (he calls his
own by name, we learn in John 10:3), turns Mary round from
death to life: a true conversion. The darkness of the early dawn,
the darkness of Mary's confusion and sorrow have lifted to light
and life.

The transformative encounter is not yet complete, and the
next verse has proved a stumbling block. It has been interpreted
in the light – or should we say the darkness? – of the misreading
of Mary Magdalene as 'fallen woman' and has been seen as a
further indictment of women as dangerous temptresses. The
command 'Do not touch' to Mary is contrasted with the permis-
sion to Thomas to touch (Jn 20:27). However, if we read with the
presupposition that Mary is a true and trusted disciple, then we
observe a different rhythm in the text. We recognise the flow
between 'Do not hold on to me.' and 'But go to my brothers and
say to them'. The apparent prohibition is linked to the commission. Mary is turned round from her preoccupation with the
past history of Jesus to the present where the *locus* of the
presence of Christ is the community.[30] We also need to link the
command back to Mary's original seeking for the dead body
and recognise that she is being drawn into a new mode of
knowing. This is why I suggested the parallel with the Emmaus
experience and the moment of insight which coincided with the
disappearance of Jesus: 'Then their eyes were opened and they
recognised him; and he vanished from their sight' (Lk 24:31).

Many artists have depicted the scene in the garden; one
familiar work is that of Titian, *Noli me Tangere* (*ca*1510-5, now in
the National Gallery, London). It has been beautifully described by John Drury as 'the transformation of love'. According to Drury, Mary's gesture of reaching out is a gesture which

changes from

reaching-to-touch into open wonder at the Lord she cannot grasp. The meaning of this momentous gesture suffuses the whole painting, where it is not just a matter of a hand, but of a whole structure of change which includes bodies and landscape.[31]

This is not just about an individual transformation but one which affects the whole social body, indeed the whole cosmos. It is a travesty to reduce the encounter between Jesus and Mary Magdalene to a private domestic scene of consolation and admonition, and to fail to see its implications as a symbolic encounter between Jesus and the Johannine community of whom Mary (like the Samaritan woman in relation to her community – Jn 4) is the representative.

Like the Samaritan woman too, Mary Magdalene is sent out: 'Mary Magdalene went and announced to the disciples, "I have seen the Lord"; and she told them he had said these things to her' (Jn 20:18). And we could easily add, 'And many believed because of her testimony' (Jn 4:39). 'The Lord has risen indeed and has appeared to Simon' (Lk 24:33) was the confirmation given to the disciples according to the Gospel of Luke; but we are given no direct record of that appearance. In contrast, in the Fourth Gospel Mary Magdalene is the first apostle to receive the Easter message and the commission to proclaim it. She communicates it and in this case the words are not taken out of her mouth and given to Peter, not then anyway![32]

So once again as we gather around Miriam's well[33] to bless and honour the memory of Mary Magdalene we shall recall her in the first place using her honoured title in the Eastern Church, Apostle to the Apostles; we shall name her as 'official apostolic witness of the resurrection',[34] we shall know her as Seeker and Searcher, we shall remember her as Woman of the Word *par excellence*, as a fitting patron of the Order of Preachers. Before we leave Mary of Magdala, I want to use my own hermeneutics of imagination here: I have a dream that future generations, having lamented the history of Magdalene laundries, will then learn of Magdalene Institutes of Preaching and Theology set up by Dominican women in the twenty-first century to train and prepare women for ministry and mission!

CONCLUSION

As we draw these thoughts together there are some threads I want to pick up and weave more closely into the tapestry. The first I have referred to already and want to underline here, and that is the importance of community. Neither Miriam nor Mary Magdalene should be isolated from their companions. Indeed, we saw that the people refused to move on until Miriam had been brought back in (Num 12:15). Although John's Gospel sets the scene of the resurrection appearance as a person-to-person encounter, that is typical of the Fourth Gospel where these figures tend to be representatives of their communities and return to them, as in the case of the Samaritan woman, who, like Mary of Magdala, has a gospel to proclaim. I stress this point because this is not about finding heroines to replace heroes but looking for alternative models of leadership, preaching and ministry for women.

We have looked at two women who have had an ambivalent history in the tradition and whose memories were distorted to serve patriarchal interests. In both cases the stories proved to be susceptible of new meanings.

I am very taken with two images used by Catherine Hilkert to talk about the role of the preacher within the Christian community. She speaks of the elders of the community as those who hold the memories and who call on the community to reflect on the treasures in their midst. The wisdom of the grandmothers of our faith is a missing wisdom in our time. So we call not just on the foremothers Miriam and Mary Magdalene, but on all those women whose stories have been forgotten, whose wisdom is neglected, that large company of 'anon'!

Hilkert's second metaphor for preaching is that of the midwife, those attending to the pulse of God at the heart of creation. As a midwife, the preacher is the one who accompanies and supports, the one who helps to bring the Word to birth.[35] I think of Miriam standing in the tradition of the Hebrew midwives Shiprah and Puah as she sought to save the child. Mary Magdalene and the Samaritan woman were entrusted to bring the Word to the community who then needed to make it their own: 'we no longer believe because of what you said' (Jn 4:42), say the townspeople, in an apparent dismissal of the woman, but in fact proving her to be a most effective preacher of the Word. She has brought people to Jesus. What strikes us about Mary Magdalene is her presence and her capacity to stay deeply, fully attuned to what was going on. She was at the cross; she was at the tomb. When the other disciples returned to their homes she was still there. Only such a person can be entrusted to give birth to the liberating Word of God.

My final thread links us back again to Miriam and to scripture scholar, Phyllis Trible, and draws us forward to anticipate the feast of the Transfiguration. In a lecture entitled 'The Transfiguration of the Mount',[36] Trible reflects on mountains as the places of holiness and terror and yet barren of women. In a wonderful exercise in the hermeneutics of imagination, or what Trible herself describes as 'risking subversion for the sake of redemption', Trible dares 'to populate the mountains with women and to ask what difference their presence makes.'[37]

For our purposes what is exciting is that the first woman she chooses to place on that mountain top is Miriam on Mount Sinai, and then later she is there with Mary Magdalene on the Mount of Transfiguration. Starting with Miriam, Trible refers to the eloquent silence of her absence and asks whether it is her gender alone which excludes her. She reminds us that when

Moses prepared the people to receive the words of the Lord, they also received the instruction 'do not go near a woman' (Ex19:15). She reminds us too of the poignant contrast between the face of Moses transfigured with the radiance of glory and the leprous face of Miriam transfigured by divine anger. Yet, in bringing her to the mountain Trible 'subverts the male mystique by honouring the counter witness of the text. Men no longer control the revelation from that mountain , and the revelation no longer excludes women.' [38]

We wrote her name into the book of wisdom, we included her in the list of valiant women but here she is placed on the holy mountain: 'Moses and Miriam, male and female God created them.'

Turning to the feast of the Transfiguration and the Gospel according to Mark we read that, 'Six days later Jesus took with him Peter and James and John, and led them up a high mountain apart, by themselves. And he was transfigured before them … And there appeared to them Elijah and Moses' (Mk 9:2,4). An all-male cast with which we are so familiar.

But what happens to our imaginative grasp of the holy when the cast extends to include women, and Miriam stands next to Moses and we remember the prophets sent before us? Does the transfiguration of Miriam's face challenge the transfiguration of the face of Jesus as Trible suggests? Can our image of God hold the image of the female? Is female flesh forever condemned to stay outside the camp, excluded from holy mountains and holy sanctuaries, or can female flesh reflect divine glory?

When Trible reflects on the merits of including Mary Magdalene, the Apostle, on the mountain, she reminds us that she figures prominently at the crucifixion and resurrection.[39] Peter finds it difficult to grasp the significance of the transfiguration and in Mark's account of the resurrection he appears only off-stage, 'Go tell his disciples and Peter … ' (Mk 16:7). In the accounts of Luke and John he goes home, having seen the empty tomb (Lk 24:11; Jn 20:10). Mary Magdalene, on the other hand, according to all the Gospel writers, stays and waits, trusting both her experience of the empty tomb and her experience of the risen Lord. Indeed, the longer ending of Mark, like the Gospel of John, credits her with an individual commission (Mk 16:9). So, to place her on the Mount of Transfiguration gives us a witness whom we can trust to read the signs rightly and open up its meaning to us. Placing her on the mountain also opens the possibility that there are not only 'beloved sons' but beloved daughters as well. Placing Mary Magdalene on the mountain with the male disciples reflects the inclusivity of the reign of God. Finally, as we stretch our imaginations to place these women here on this holy mount, we break the doomed connection between maleness and holiness, and femaleness and sinfulness, and allow women as well as men to be fully christomorphic.

I am going to finish with the words of Phyllis Trible who is herself a valiant woman of the word and has been a wisdom guide on this journey:

> Let the word go forth from the primeval abyss to the dome of heaven that women in scripture have moved to the mountains of revelation. On this sacred turf they dare to meet God and so remove another boundary to the full participation of women in the biblical witness. These women begin the transfiguration of the mount to the end that the divine presence encounters all sorts and conditions of people. If this be heresy, make the best of it. [40]

The Space In Between
– Mission as Reconciliation

JOHN D'ARCY MAY

Farewelling a colleague recently, an American Mennonite who has spent over twenty years in Ireland, studying Irish history and doing innovative research on overcoming sectarianism,[1] it occurred to me that I had long thought of him and his wife as missionaries – but in a sense quite different from the Irish missionaries who went out to distant continents to make converts to Christianity. While his wife worked with disadvantaged children in a depressed area of Dublin, my colleague endured the frustrations of trying to get groups of Catholics and Protestants in the polarised urban ghettos and country towns of Northern Ireland and the border counties to come together and stay together as they confronted their stereotypes of one another. His work was not so much evangelisation as reconciliation, and that, I now realise, made him a missionary in a new – we might say 'post-modern' – sense.

He might also be called a post-colonial missionary. The legacy of Christianity's liaisons with colonialism has made 'mission' synonymous with the destruction of indigenous cultures and the imposition of Western values and institutions, an historical mistake the West should be ashamed of. While companies and other organisations, already oblivious of this heritage, frame their 'mission statements', mission has become almost unmentionable in many theological circles. The 'discovery' of what was to Europeans a New World by Columbus in 1492 marked the beginning of an era in which evangelisation was closely bound up with *conquista*. Once the Protestant powers of Europe joined the race for colonies, nationalism and denominationalism marched arm in arm through much of Asia,

all of Africa and across the Pacific. In the footsteps of the
Catholic Spanish and the Calvinist Dutch, the Lutheran Ger-
mans, Catholic French and Anglican or Free Church British
carved out ecclesiastical enclaves just as their colonial sponsors
had carved out trading enclaves. The latter sought raw materi-
als and markets while the former tried to win 'souls'.

Evangelisation in such a context became identical with
'spatialisation': Europeans re-imagined the world as contigu-
ous territories owned and controlled by them, and these in turn
created the spaces for evangelisation. The nations and Churches
thus created were meant to be carbon-copies of their European
exemplars, but the states that eventually emerged after painful
and often violent struggles for independence were 'soft states'
(Gunnar Myrdal), flaunting the trappings of democracy and the
rule of law but economically dependent on their former colonial
masters and politically unstable.

When I used this term at a farewell conference for a German
Lutheran colleague from Papua New Guinea he interjected:
'Soft Churches?', and I found myself saying, why not? Catholic
missions, by and large, remain largely Western in personnel
and appearance, but Protestant missions were usually intended
to become 'localised' autonomous Churches from the start, and
the ways in which they achieved this were often pioneering.[2]
But the resulting indigenous Churches, to the extent that they
are truly indigenous, often find themselves riven by internal
conflicts over authenticity and administration and in tension
with their overseas 'mother Churches', who still contribute
much of their financial support.[3] If 'globalisation' means the
definitive domination of the world by Western mentalities and
technologies, then the great Catholic and Protestant missionary
eras now look like a kind of Christian globalisation; but these
eras are now over. The time in which mission meant maximis-
ing the Gospel's sphere of influence by starting from a securely
held 'centre' – the Christianities of Europe and the West – is no

more. Europe itself is now increasingly recognised as 'mission territory', whether that means the invasion of Eastern Europe by evangelistic groups (even the re-ordering of dioceses by Rome was interpreted by the Russian Orthodox as proselytism![4]) or the proliferation of *ad hoc* mini-Churches and neo-pagan revivals in the midst of Western European religious pluralism. The liasion with colonialism has been replaced by complicity with capitalism as American Pentecostals and Evangelicals 'market' Christianity using all the sophisticated techniques of media-driven fundraising. Globalisation as spatial expansion is now being complemented by occupation of the 'virtual space' through which finance, information and entertainment flow; evangelisation, too, is now being transformed from physical presence into virtual presence in the 'real virtuality' of the global public forum.[5]

Yet we must never forget that old-fashioned evangelisation did 'proclaim good news', transforming individual lives and pacifying hostile communities. With great personal sacrifice the missionaries did 'bear witness' to a freely given love that saves and a peace that heals, as happened among the warring tribes of New Guinea and elsewhere in the Pacific Islands and as continues to happen today through communities of reconciliation like Corrymeela and Glencree in Ireland or Sant' Egidio and the Focolarini of Chiara Lubich internationally. It was precisely the 'success' of evangelisation during the great missionary eras that made Christianity a 'world religion', but this has also left us a legacy of 'ecumenical' problems in the original meaning of the word: problems that result from Christianity's polycentric presence throughout the whole inhabited world (*oikoumene*). Christianities are in conflict and Christians are estranged along lines which have little to do with the classical ecclesiastical divisions (Latin West, Orthodox East; Roman Catholicism, varieties of Protestantism). The white/black, rich/poor, centre/periphery polarities are a direct inheritance of the missionary past, while those between men / women, straight / gay and healthy / disabled have become Church-dividing factors in modern contexts. As a result, while postcolonial conflicts continue in post-missionary Churches – the divisions in the Methodist Church of Fiji over the presence in government of ethnic Indians who are either Hindu or Muslim is a dramatic example – the reverse flow of Christians from former mission countries back to the West creates a proliferation of new Churches such as the Black Churches in Britain and America or the ethnic immigrant Churches in Australia and New Zealand. Meanwhile, the 'parent' Churches threaten to tear themselves apart over issues which leave their missionary offspring shaking their heads uncomprehendingly (the ordination of gays and lesbians in the Anglican Church in England and the Episcopalian Church in America or the Uniting Church in Australia is a case in point, but there are many other such issues in the fields of bioethics and medical ethics).

What is the answer to these new challenges from a missionary point of view? There are those who would redefine mission as development, relief work, health care or education in order to avoid any implication of proselytism. But in these fields there is every danger that the old missionary problem of imposing one's values and institutions on those one wants to help will repeat itself in secular form. The avoidance of conversion by coercion (*Bekehrung* or proselytism) does not preclude aiming at conversion as *metanoia* (*Umkehr* or a radical and liberating change of heart and mind). But today such radical conversion need not imply abandoning one religious identity in order to take on another, 'leaving' one Church or religion in order to 'join' a different one; it may also take the form of dual or even multiple religious belonging, so that one hears of 'Catholic Evangelicals', 'Hindu Christians' or 'Buddhist Jews', just as there have always been many people of indeterminate religious identity in China and Japan.[6]

The 'space' of mission, I would suggest, is no longer the geographical space of territorial expansion or even the virtual space of the new electronic media, but the space 'in between' those who are estranged or at enmity, even in violent conflict. Mission is happening in the interstices of the global system, in spaces where, given patience, skilful mediation and God's grace, miracles of reconciliation can occur. In Australia, 'reconciliation' has long since established itself on the political agenda as the great national collaborative task of healing the hurt of white invasion, cultural dispossession and family separation; the South African Truth and Reconciliation Commission has become an international landmark, not least because it combined indigenous and Christian ways of confronting the past, making restitution and in some cases forgiving; the process of reconciliation after eight years of civil war on the Papua New Guinea island of Bougainville has yielded moving examples of the same combination of indigenous and Christian inspiration as well as resulting in almost complete disarmament; in Northern Ireland the process of reconciliation, both political and religious, though far from complete, has reached the point where it can be comprehensively studied in a comparative framework.[7]

Reconciliation in such contexts – and consequently mission, if my hypothesis is correct – can only be conceived as radical non-violence. It is the witness given to a love that suffers rather than requite injustice and that can thus inspire gratuitous forgiveness. It is a witness that can counteract the logic of reciprocal retribution, whether in the 'payback' system of Melanesian cultures or the cult of revenge in the post-Christian West. In a post-colonial, post-missionary situation, mission has been set free from the constraints and compromises of the past to become the witness of reconciliation. Gandhi's 'soul force' (*satyagraha*, literally 'dwelling in the truth' by refusing to retaliate), and Martin Luther King's non-violent struggle for civil rights are its precursors; the endemic violence of the conflicts in the Middle East, the Balkans and Northern Ireland are testimonies to what can happen in its absence.

Mission as reconciliation, like politics, is always local and context-specific: there is no such thing as forgiveness 'in general'! Yet it is not just a matter of reconciling individuals – often ethnic or religious groups are involved, as in Indian 'communalism' – and it often has to come to grips with global factors such as fundamentalism and what has been called the 'market state' (Archbishop Rowan Williams in his 2003 Dimbleby Lecture). The love to which mission as reconciliation bears witness must be shown to transcend the twin idols of *Blut und Boden*: the 'blood' of ethnic identity regarded as a guarantee of superiority, and the 'soil' of territorial attachment (such as the Land of Israel or the sacred ground of Kosovo; it was the indigenous ideology of land as a sacred inheritance, *taukei*, that so bedevilled the Christian response to the 1987 military coups in Fiji and the subsequent constitutional crisis). Precisely as local, this witness must also be communicable to the whole *oikoumene* and must be able to be acknowledged as Christian witness to Gospel values: it is witness to the whole Church (*kath' holon*, 'catholic'). It is in fact neither more nor less than 'realised catholicity', the full living out of the redemptive love celebrated in the Eucharist by all Christians in every place.[8]

The globalised public space of post-modernity, then, created in the course of colonisation and its accompanying evangelisation of almost the entire globe, offers plenty of scope for the ministry of reconciliation at both local and global levels. Europe, whose wars and revolutions repeatedly spilled over into the rest of the world during the twentieth century's 'long war' (1914-1989), has now structured itself as a zone of peace in which military conflict among members of the European Union is increasingly unthinkable (though Greece and Turkey are an embarrassment, the future role of the Balkan states is uncertain, and Northern Ireland always was and still is a European conflict). But if we look around the rest of the world, it is remarkable how many of the endemic conflicts whose protracted violence seems to defy mediation, have their roots in European colonial practices, now augmented by American neo-imperialism and the hegemonic ambitions of states like Indonesia and China.

It is of course well beyond the scope of individual missionaries and their para-church organisations to mediate effectively at this level; even the Catholic Church, with its curious combination of diplomacy and theology, is only able to intervene sporadically, as in the Pope's attempts to prevent war in Iraq. But we must not be daunted by the size of this task, because it is normally not in the public space where international relations and interreligious dialogue intersect, but in the spaces *in between* the great players and the embittered combatants, the perpetrators and their victims, that the ministry of reconciliation can be most effective. Gandhi once remarked: 'The only people on earth who do not see Christ and his teachings as non-violent are Christians'.[9] It is precisely in post-missionary conflict situations that the realisation dawns on us that the Gospel is in fact a testament of non-violence. And this violence is not restricted to civil wars, terrorism and the interventions of great powers. At all levels in all societies violence seems to be spreading as alienated individuals and disaffected groups lash out in frustration at those who seem to 'have it all' whereas they can only nurse their grievances. In such a situation of generalised insecurity, both local and global, the ministry of reconciliation – under certain conditions yet to be defined – becomes the most distinctive form of witness to the Gospel. But in order to offer this witness credibly, we Christians have a lot of soul-searching and historical homework to do.

The act of conversion itself, the attempt to interfere with well-formed individual and cultural identities and bring about change, whether by coercion or persuasion, is now seen to be not just the precursor but the primordial form of violence.[10] Increasingly, 'the monotheisms', as the Abrahamic traditions of Jews, Christians and Muslims are somewhat loosely called, are accused of being intrinsically violent because they worship a violent God.[11] Here Christians need to embark on painful deconstructions of some very basic convictions. The concept of God as an all-powerful sanctioner of righteous violence has become the idol of powerful Churches and now underpins what my colleague Bill McSweeney calls 'the theology of American foreign policy'. The notion of substitutionary sacrifice – that human guilt is so great that nothing less than the violent death of God's own Son in our place can expiate it by appeasing the divine anger – does not so much transform as succumb to the ideology of retaliatory violence.

These tasks in turn stir up whole nests of neglected missiological questions: can indigenous notions of retributive justice be Christianised by assimilating them to the sacrifice of Christ, or does this amount to a 're-paganising' of the Christian theology of redemptive sacrifice?[12] The argument turns around two difficult and controversial issues, one anthropological, the other theological: whether the ritual killings found in Melanesian and most other indigenous cultures are in fact 'sacrifices', and whether Jesus' submission to the violence of the cross was in fact the sacrifice that transcends all sacrifice and breaks the cycle of retaliatory violence once and for all.[13] We cannot pursue these questions here, but they show the depths to which the theology of reconciliation takes us. In the post-colonial context both the Churches' long-standing commitment to the doctrine of just war and the witness of the historic 'peace Churches' (Mennonites, Quakers, Amish) are being re-evaluated.[14]

In confronting these issues it is important to be clear that reconciliation is not a 'soft option': it is not a substitute for justice but presupposes it, and it involves us in the extremely sensitive question of forgiveness. Reconciliation in no way implies suppressing the memory of violence and injustice, but rather insists on victims and perpetrators alike confronting the truth of past and present injustice in order to build a new relationship. Reconciliation is thus not an alternative to liberation but a crucial step on the way towards it; indeed, reconciliation could become the new form of liberation theology, for it is forgiveness that sets us free to shape our future together.[15]

Nor is reconciliation to be confused with professional mediation, the management of conflict with the help of experts who stand outside it. Such attempts can have the effect of antagonising the combatants still further, for what drives their violence is usually the deep-seated fear that they will be alienated from their traditions and their identity be destroyed.[16] The work of reconciliation begins with the conviction that the parties to a conflict, no matter how bitter and violent, themselves possess the resources to master their fears and dismantle their stereotypes, if only the grace of forgiveness can be allowed to penetrate the space in between their antagonisms and grievances.[17]

At the core of the theology of reconciliation – and consequently of the new missiology – is the delicate problem of forgiveness. There can be no real reconciliation which transforms conflict and transcends violence without forgiveness. But who can ask forgiveness? Anyone who has been really hurt, even in a family feud or a misunderstanding between colleagues, let alone those who have lost loved ones or sustained injuries in violent conflicts, knows how immeasurably difficult it can be to forgive. Faced with the impossibility of forgiveness, it is not enough to say 'Don't worry, God's grace will heal your wounds and open your heart.' There is no place for what Dietrich Bonhoeffer called 'cheap grace' in the mysterious process that leads to forgiveness. Indeed, the Catholic Church's misuse of the 'forgiveness of sins' as an instrument of power played a central part in the Reformation revolt, which led Protestants to conceive of both sin and forgiveness 'vertically', as an affair between the individual sinner and God. What was lost was an understanding of the social dimension of forgiveness and the need to involve both victim and perpetrator, with priority being given to the victim.[18] If repentance on the part of perpetrators is to go beyond mere restitution to acknowledge responsibility and set about rebuilding relationships for a better future, conditions must be created in which victims can forgive, though the act of forgiveness itself is beyond human control and marks the entry point of divine grace into the negative space of antagonism and grievance, shame and guilt. The risk is that, when the pain of shame encounters the pain of grievance, the request for forgiveness does not necessarily call forth forgiveness, and the act of forgiveness does not necessarily result in repentance.

Yet it is at this point of greatest sensitivity that the true dimensions of the new missionary task become apparent, for the missionary as reconciler must aim at nothing less than a positive new beginning based on a promise, a new covenant, not just between individuals but in certain circumstances between ethnic groups and social classes. 'Re-membering' now implies not just facing the past but restoring community. It is the inability to cope with 'deep remembering' on this scale that makes politics so aggressive and reactionary, as the Australian government's refusal to apologise to Aboriginal people for the hurt done them in the past eloquently testifies. Yet such reconciliation is happening, usually in local contexts such as Bougainville or Northern Ireland, but on such a scale that local reconciliation is already a significant political factor in the new global public sphere.

In speaking this way about forgiveness, about the love that 'liberates and redeems by not requiting evil, and thereby bears witness to the fact that '[i]f God really could not forgive, then

God would actually be powerless against the law of retribution',[19] we find ourselves very close to the ideal of the Bodhisattva in Buddhism. The Bodhisattva is an enlightened person who renounces the final consummation in the peace of *nirvana* out of compassion for all suffering creatures. The Bodhisattva radiates the compassionate love (*metta-karunâ*) of a purified mind to all, perpetrators and victims, evil and good, human and non-human, because all are ultimately interdependent; in the words of Thich Nhat Hanh, we all 'inter-are' and no-one can stand outside or above another. The extent to which this compassion includes the love that forgives could be fruitfully explored in the Buddhist-Christian dialogue.

It now becomes apparent that the question of reconciliation and forgiveness as the new form of mission inevitably throws up the whole problem of the dialogue of religions. In a world now fully aware of its religious plurality it is obvious to all but the most benighted fundamentalists that no one religious tradition on its own can meet the challenge of reconciliation on the scale we have indicated. The fact that so much violent conflict is between religions or is fuelled by religious convictions is enough in itself to discredit the religions as agents of reconciliation. Yet it is the religions that have traditionally offered the transcendent perspectives, the moral teachings and the exemplary practitioners of non-violence, all of which makes them indispensable in defining peace, enabling forgiveness and bringing about reconciliation, both globally and locally. Many of the world's 'militants for peace' are religiously inspired, from informal groups and locally based movements (such as the Corrymeela Community, the Community of Sant' Egidio, the International Network of Engaged Buddhists or the Fellowship of Reconciliation) to transnational institutions with the resources of the Roman Catholic Church, the World Council of Churches or the World Conference on Religion and Peace.[20]

Some of the qualities required of peacemakers, however,

whether as external-disinterested or internal-partisan media-
tors, present a considerable challenge when we transpose them
to the religions themselves with their various sects and denomi-
nations: acknowledgement of the mediator's vulnerability and
self-doubt; discernment of the interpersonal values of one's
own culture and others'; the conviction that these values have
peacemaking potential, no matter how passionate the rage and
fanaticism of extremist groups. These are the ingredients of
what John Paul Lederach calls 'elicitive peacemaking', but they
must be seen in the context of the crucial dilemma of religions
in conflict as discerned by Marc Gopin: the authentic expression
of one's own religiosity *versus* unconditional respect for others';
the need to be unique *versus* the need to integrate.[21] One could
hardly express more pointedly the ways in which 'mission' and
'dialogue' intersect. In order to be credible, the dialogue of
religions must be intrinsically non-violent. Not the dualism of
Crusade *versus* Jihad, but the non-dualism of repentance and
forgiveness in reconciliation, perhaps even to the point of
multiple religious belonging in a world that is both global and
plural, is the new missionary horizon.

Renewing the Dominican Vision – 'A Passion of Possibility'

MARY O'DRISCOLL, O.P.

There is a poem by the Danish philosopher, Søren Kierkegaard, called 'The Moment' which has the following lines:

If I could wish for something,
I would wish for neither wealth nor power,
but for the passion of possibility;
I would wish only for an eye which, eternally young,
eternally burns with the longing to see possibility.[1]

I would like to reflect with you today on the 'passion of possibility' which Kierkegaard talks about in his poem; and I would like to do so in terms of our theme 'Renewing the Dominican Vision'. What might it mean for us, Dominicans of today, from north, south, east and west, to have the passion of possibility stirring within us anew? What might it mean for us to view our Dominican mission in the world with eyes which, in Kierkegaard's words, are eternally young, eternally burning with the longing to see possibility? I am sure that we would all wish for those kinds of eyes, for to have them is to be fired with a passion for greater and greater possibilities, possibilities that enable us to enter into a deeper contemplative relationship with God, and at the same time, to be more convinced bearers of the good news in our contemporary world.

It is not difficult, I imagine, to understand what we have in mind when we talk of the passion of possibility burning within us. It means surely that we are continually on the look-out for ways to push out the boundaries of what is possible in our own lives, as well as in our communities and congregations, and in our world, all for the sake of the coming of the reign of God. We want to make what may seem impossible, possible – a deep contemplative peace within us, a new vision and enthusiasm in our communities, and in our society, justice for all, no more homelessness, enough food for all to enjoy, the end of discrimination of all kinds, a cessation of violence in all its terrible manifestations, a respect and care for the beautiful universe in which we live.

We could go on and on, for we all have our dreams of what is possible through the extravagant, empowering gifts of the Spirit. The one, above all, who shows us, and who lived out in his own life, the passion of possibility is Jesus, God-with-us. He is the one whose eye was eternally young, eternally burning with the longing to see possibility. He healed and taught, loved and wept, and finally gave his life so that the ultimate and fullest possibility would be open to all. And his gift to us is the Spirit who makes all things new.

Gustavo Gutierrez, in an address to the World Social Forum in Brazil, this year, quotes a line from a Spanish poet: 'Sometimes dreams are not dreamt anymore, and become reality'. [2] It is the passion of possibility that can move dreams into reality.

But, what is 'passion'? We could begin by describing it as the opposite of apathy or indifference. But, of course, it is more than that. Passion is love. Maybe we can say that passion is that quality in our love that is not content to stand still, but rather is convinced that more is possible. Those who are in love can best tell us what passion is. The gospel of Mark states that after Jesus heard the voice from heaven: 'You are my beloved Son; my favour rests on you', he was driven by the Spirit into the desert (Mk1:11-12). That's what passion does; it drives us. Even more precisely, when our passion is for the things of God, as Jesus' obviously was, it is the Spirit that drives us forward. When passion takes hold of a person, there is no stopping him/her. We think of Paul's cry to the Corinthians: 'Woe is me if I do not preach the gospel', or, as another translation has it: 'I am under compulsion and I should be in trouble if I failed to preach the good news … ' (1 Cor 9:16). He just had to preach. The Spirit was pushing him. Do we have that kind of passion stirring within us? Is there any dream that I am so seized by that I feel myself compelled to do everyting I can to make it a reality? If so, I know what passion is.

Throughout the Scriptures we have many examples of the passion of possibility, through the gift of the renewing Spirit, pushing, stretching, challenging women in their mission to make seemingly impossible dreams possible: magnificent women like Miriam who bravely defied the Pharaoh's command that all male Hebrew babies be killed; Judith, that beautiful courageous woman who liberated her people from the Assyrian siege at the risk of her own life; the Canaanite woman who challenged Jesus' understanding of what was possible, and in doing so, helped to enlarge the focus of his ministry; Mary Magdalene whose tremendous love for Jesus opened up the possibility for her to proclaim the Resurrection to the disciples. Above all there is Mary of Nazareth who was confronted with the most impossible situation anyone could imagine. 'How can this happen?' she asked, and the answer she received, 'All things are possible to God', expanded her passion for the possible until it coincided with God's passion for the possible.

DOMINICAN PASSION DOWN THE CENTURIES

The Dominican dream was born of Dominic's 'passion of possibility'. As he stood on the hill of Fanjeaux, that place which we call the 'Seignadou', and looked down at the surrounding country, what did he see? Yes, he saw the plains below with their crops and scattered houses; he saw the roads leading in all directions taking travellers away and bringing them back, but he also saw a people being led astray, a people longing for the truth. 'What can I do?' he asked himself over and over again as he stood at this place of crossroads, his eyes burning with a longing to see a better possibility for the people of Southern France. As Simon Tugwell puts it:

He was a man who wept
And in his tears glistened ... love,
Human and tender; human because divine
Divine because wrung from prayer, from an agony of truth.
'Ah Lord, what will become of sinners?'[3]

In his first faltering steps towards making the seemingly impossible possible, Dominic gathered a band of companions whose eyes were given a new vision.

Among these companions were women. Vicaire reminds us that Dominic was always quick to see the particular possibilities for evangelization which women offered, and immediately included them in his preaching band.[4] We hear, for example, of the women of Fanjeaux who were important teachers among the Albigensians, and who, on being converted, stood side by side with Dominic bringing the good news of God's love and care to others. These early women formed a kind of missionary community. They had no common place of abode, but they had a common passion, namely, to proclaim the gospel.[5] Later as Dominic moved from place to place in his itinerant preaching, he continued to share his vision with women, enabling them to have new eyes burning with possibilities.

Right through the history of our Order, long after Dominic's death, we encounter marvellous women, imbued with the Dominican spirit, whose eyes were eternally young. In discovering the identities and achievements of many of these, I have been amazed and delighted to find that the times when they most often came to the fore, pushing the boundaries of possibility further, were times of crisis and suffering, times when the forces of violence and injustice were raging. Again and again, we discover them stepping into a seemingly hopeless situation, offering a new possibility that not only changed but also transformed it.

We think of the Slav, Zedislava of Lemberk, who in the thirteenth century was concerned about the poverty and the ignorance of the people in Eastern Europe and who, on meeting the friars, Hyacinth and Ceslaus of Poland, saw the possibilities which the newly-founded Order of Preachers offered. Her biographer tells us that she was 'enchanted with its possibilities', and threw herself into its apostolic life, teaching catechism, caring for the poor and visiting prisoners. When she was canonized in 1995, she was hailed as the Dominican woman who evangelized the Slav world. We remember also the young woman in Italy who was born blind and a hunchback, Margaret of Castello. Professed as a lay Dominican, she seized the possibility offered to her in her own pain and deformity to comfort and encourage the troubled people in her hometown to such an extent that she continues to be regarded as the patron and friend of handicapped people everywhere.

If we are looking for Dominican women whose eyes longed to see possibility, perhaps the person who most readily springs to mind is Catherine of Siena. If ever there was anyone who understood the Dominican vocation, and consequently burned with a passion to preach the gospel, it was she. The day she made her profession in the Order was a day that enlarged the possibilities of all Dominicans. Of her, the Master of the Order, Aniceto Fernandez, wrote: 'Into Catherine the whole soul of Dominic passed'.[6] Her positive and penetrating insights into God's goodness and human dignity fired in her an insatiable desire to tell people how precious and beautiful they were in God's eyes. Her contemplative and deep relationship with God in the midst of much activity has encouraged many to live, like her, in their 'cell of self-knowledge'. Her fearless courage and infectious enthusiasm in preaching the gospel in a very troubled century have expanded for many their appreciation of unexplored possibilities open to women. In the words of John Paul II, she 'dived into the thick of the ecclesiastical and social issues of her time',[7] refusing to resign herself in the face of the suffering and division in the Europe of her day. Catherine threw herself into this impossible situation, not to prolong it, not to use the methods of violence and force that were favoured, but to bring about a new possibility – peace and reconciliation.

She, however, had her own struggle to get to this point. When she first realised that she was being asked to do things on the social and political front, as well as for the Church, things not done previously by women, she addressed God in prayer. ' I'm only a woman. Surely, I'm not meant to play such a public role!' And God gave her her answer, an echo of what was said to Mary at the Incarnation: 'All things are possible to me. Go! Do the work I have entrusted to you. I will be with you.'[8] With that encouragement ringing in her ears, Catherine went forth, discovering all over the place new possibilities to bring the good news of God's love and compassion to countless people in all ranks of life.

In the same century as Catherine, in the Rhineland, other Dominican women's eyes were burning with the longing to see new contemplative possibilities for themselves and others. Some of their names are familiar to us – Margaret Ebner, Christine Ebner, Elizabeth Stägel, Adelaide Langmann – but there were many more living in the Dominican monasteries scattered throughout the Rhineland. With their brothers, including Eckhart, Tauler, Suso, through their lives of prayer and study, they arrived at a new understanding and a new way of describing, the path to union with God. These women are credited with playing a tremendous role in developing a new kind of mysticism open to everyone.[9] In so doing, they have helped countless people down to our own time to enter more deeply into the spiritual life.

Another Dominican woman whose heart expanded with a

longing to make the impossible possible was Rose of Lima. Moved by tremendous compassion for the poor in Peru she spent her life caring for them. She made such a difference to their abject situation that, to this day, she is honoured as 'mother of the poor'.

In China in the seventeenth century, there were two Dominican women, both named Catherine, from very different social backgrounds whose zeal enlarged the possibilities of life and work for many of their contemporaries. Between them, they ran study circles and lived an intensely Dominican life in the mountains.

Over in France, in the seventeenth century a young woman called Marie Pousepin was so moved by the poverty of her countrywomen and men that she brought together a band of enthusiastic women to care for the needs of the poor. She was so successful that when she was beatified in 1994 she was given the title, 'social apostle of charity'. She is the founder of the Dominican Sisters of the Presentation who have travelled all over the world with the good news of God's love for the little ones, the marginalised, the poor.

Indeed, we could go on and on lifting up great women of past centuries whose Dominican passion urged them to be more, to see more and do more than they had previously thought possible.

IN OUR OWN CONGREGATIONS

At this symposium we have been hearing about our own great women of the past, beginning with Mary Lynch and Julian Nolan who fled to Spain at the time of Cromwell's persecution in Ireland, and who in 1686, when they themselves were elderly, brought Dominican life for women back to their own country. They have been followed, as we have seen, by magnificent women who have pioneered with great courage and determination new forms of education in Ireland, making the seemingly impossible possible on many unexpected fronts; and by wave after missionary wave of valiant women in the nineteenth and twentieth centuries, whose Dominican sense of the possible urged them to leave their native land in order to bring the gospel message to far-away places – to Australia, New Zealand, South Africa, Latin America, North America, Portugal. There were in all nine separate foundations outside Ireland. In the story of each one of these, we can marvel at the spirit of the Sisters, who for love of Christ and the people they came to serve, were ingenious in making the impossible possible even when they had to contend with all kinds of hardships, deep loneliness, misunderstandings with local bishops and clergy, frightening poverty and insecurity. Their accounts, which fortunately have been preserved, of difficult and perilous journeys by sea from Ireland to their respective destinations, would make even the most stouthearted quail. But these first Irish Dominican women-missionaries were undaunted, intrepid, passionate, continually driven forward in their desire to spread the reign of God. One record from this time notes that 'the countries of adoption were new, the climate was trying, help was not easy to find, and money was not to spare'.[10] Yet, confronted with the needs of those around them, the Sisters attempted the impossible and in very many cases made it possible. The passion of possibility had seared into each of their hearts an insatiable longing to spread the good news of God's love and mercy far and wide on our earth. What a magnificent witness to trust in God and to Spirit-led drivenness is revealed in their stories!

May I be permitted to pause for a few moments in South Africa to relate just one story of how Dominican Sisters made the seemingly impossible possible? Many people in this room saw the story unfolding. It concerns the dramatic ending of apartheid in school education. The year was 1976 and up to this point in South Africa, the regime of strict apartheid dictated that black and white students would be educated separately. However, a dilemma arose for the government when it set up diplomatic relations with independent black states, for now black ambassadors and their families came to live in South Africa and they needed good education. The Catholic private schools for whites were asked to accept the black children from diplomatic families. Sr Genevieve Hickey, a feisty, courageous Dominican woman in Cape Town, was alert to the possibility which presented itself in this request and refused to accept the diplomats' children if other black students could not enter white schools as well. The authorities refused, but the Dominicans ignored them, opening their schools to all black students. The government's reaction came swiftly: 'Get the black students out of your schools or we will close them.' The Dominicans replied: 'You can close our schools, but we won't'. This called the government's bluff, and thus through that brave action the process of racial integration in education began in South Africa. 'Dominican nuns smash apartheid' the international headlines proclaimed. They were accompanied by the Mercy Sisters, the Marist Brothers, and other religious, as well as by Anglican educationalists. In all, 150 schools were involved. This daring gospel move gave courage to the Catholic bishops who spoke out publicly against all forms of discrimination in the country.

So far, we have been reflecting on other women, among them our own great foremothers, admiring and rejoicing in their passion for the possible. However, that is not enough. Wonderful as it is to belong to such a throng of remarkable women, we cannot rest in the knowledge of what they have done. We have to ask ourselves what are we being asked to be and to do now? How can we revitalise the Dominican vision today? What passion of possibility can stretch, push and enlarge our spirits? Each of us personally, and as part of a community, will answer these questions in her own particular way. In doing so, we will

Dominican Sisters
New Zealand

Common threads connect the six panels: New Zealand's natural beauty (note the tiny paua shells in each), education ministry especially among deaf children, and continuing mission journeys to other places.

Congregation of St Mary,
New Orleans

This hand-woven rug highlights academic education as the original form of the Sisters' Dominican mission in Louisiana, from which other ministries have developed – justice promotion, retreat work and preaching.

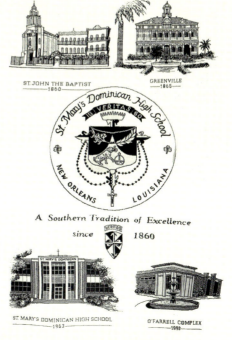

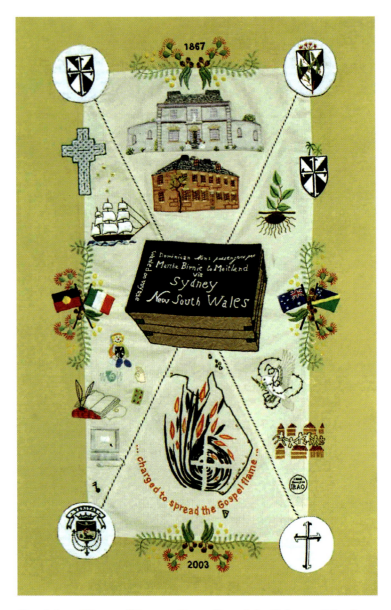

Dominican Sisters of Eastern Australia and the Solomon Islands

The motifs are suggestive of the Dominican mission of preaching the gospel, diverse educational ministries and pioneering journeys. We note the first sisters' travel chest in the centre, which is now in the Congregation's Heritage Centre.

take into account our own strengths and weaknesses, our gifts and limitations, our less than perfect personalities and temperaments, our hopes and fears, and the circumstances in which we live. But we will also be open to the Holy Spirit's gifts of newness and loving passion. It is certain that answer these questions we must, if we are to help to transform our world and universe and bring them to their fullest potential.

LOCAL AND UNIVERSAL

Our Dominican charism is ever ancient (at least in the sense that it goes back to the thirteenth century), but within it, it holds the seeds of ever-newness. It is not something static or frozen like a block of ice in a religious or historical deep-freeze; rather it is something fluid, like liquid, always holding within it new possibilities. It is therefore always 'becoming' at the same time as it remains the same. But, unless we allow it to develop and adapt in the different cultures and situations in which it finds itself, it will not be able to survive.

Some years ago, the friars held an international conference on Formation in the Order. As part of the conference, friars from different continents and different cultures were asked to respond to the following question: 'What impact has Dominican life on your country and culture?' Each answered this question as well as he could. It was, however, Albert Nolan's answer which was the most far-reaching and prophetic. He replied: 'We can talk of the impact of Dominican formation on Africa, but we need also to explore the impact of Africa on Dominican formation. Our charism will not have a significant impact on Africa, unless we allow Africa with its profound spiritual traditions, its deep sense of community and its endless experience of suffering, to influence our understanding of what it means to be Dominican'.

This answer carries within it a challenge to all of us. If we wish to renew and revitalise our Dominican charism, we need to allow it to interact with and be shaped by the cultural, historical, political, social and ecclesial realities in which it is being lived. It doesn't exist, and will not survive, in a vacuum. As Marie-Dominique Chenu states, the world in which we live is the the only place where our Dominican vocation takes on meaning. From its inception, the one Dominican charism has grown and developed in new ways precisely because people have dared to live it in their particular circumstances. Thomas Aquinas, Catherine of Siena, Bartolomé de las Casas, Magdalen of Nagasaki, Henri Lacordaire, Susanna of Armenia, are all witnesses to this truth.

A wonderful illustration in our times of the new possibilities, local and universal, which the Dominican charism holds is the formation of Dominican Sisters International (DSI). Before its foundation in 1995, the dominant question for Dominican Sisters was: 'How shall we, as separate congregations, continue to exist as we move into the future?' We were concerned about our own survival. Now, the dominant question is: 'How can we know, support and appreciate one another across our different congregations as we try to live out our Dominican vocation together in this present world with all its pain and all its challenge?' Delving into that question has already stirred the passion of possibility in many. DSI has made the up-to-now impossible, possible. With its emphasis on the feminine impulse to develop relationships and make connections, it is bringing Sisters together to celebrate new life, to encourage and help one another in our different fields, to move forward positively into the future, to talk to and support one another across continental lines, and to be at home with one another. DSI belongs to all Dominican Sisters wherever they are in the world. At the moment it is comprised of 32,000 women belonging to 165 congregations. One congregation is as big as 3,500 members; another is as small as five members.

DOMINICAN LONGING TODAY

Today, we celebrate the feast of the Transfiguration when the divine possibility for all of us was glimpsed in Jesus' transformed, radiant appearance (Mk 9:2-10). At the Transfiguration, the disciples were given new sight which enabled them to see this possibility. This event marked a further stage in their journey with Jesus. From then on, they saw things differently. Peter, in one of his Letters, reflecting on the Transfiguration, refers to it as 'a lamp for lighting a way through the dark' (2 Pet 1:19). We need such a lamp for lighting up our way in our own dark times when the Dominican vision has perhaps become dim or is hidden behind a cloud.

I would now like to put some questions to all of us, questions which may, in a small way, help to light up our way into the future.

Firstly, are we being summoned to express in new ways the charism of preaching which is at the core of our Dominican vocation? All of us are called to proclaim the good news and to be good news whoever and wherever we are. How do we as women interpret this call? At the General Chapter held in Bologna in 1998, the Order was asked to take seriously the question of how the charism of preaching belongs to Dominican women as well as to Dominican men, from a theological as well as an ecclesiological perspective. This question is of vital importance to everyone of us, and therefore any way in which we can be involved in exploring it, is a way in which we can help to make the impossible possible for one another. A moment when the passion of possibility for preaching took hold of a young Sister in Slovakia is encapsulated in the remark she made after a recent course on Dominican life: 'I couldn't believe my ears when I heard these words: "You may be dispensed from preaching, but you can never be exempt." I realised for the first time what it means to be responsible for the Word of God that I hold in my hands'. We are reminded that at the beginning of the

Order, a convent was called a 'sacred preaching.' Are there new ways in which we can help to make our communities 'sacred preachings'? Have we the will to stretch the call that we have all received to preach the gospel so that in this twenty-first century it opens for us new possibilities, in season and out of season (cf 2 Tim 4:2)?

Secondly, as part of renewing the Dominican charism, are we, like Catherine, being called to be peacemakers and reconcilers in places where there are conflicts and violence? In Northern Ireland, we have seen the difference women have made in the peace negotiations. From Rwanda there are some moving stories of how women tried to stop the genocide, even to the extent of going against allegiance to their own tribes, whether Hutu or Tutsie. In general, women revolt strenuously against the futility, the senseless waste of life and the utter cruelty of war. Research has shown that in countries where women play a very large part in public life, for example, in Scandinavia or Canada, there is consistently a greater interest in conflict resolution and reconciliation than in other societies. Have we a part to play in this?

Thirdly, are we convinced that the Dominican vision will never be renewed and given new possibilities if we do not share it with our lay associates, colleagues, successors in our schools and colleges, our past students, and with the laity in general? Are we passionate enough about this vision to regard it as too precious a gift to squander or to wrap in a napkin and keep hidden, just because our own numbers are diminishing? If we are, we have to ask ourselves a further practical question: What are we doing, in our countries, to ensure that the Dominican charism lives on?

Fourthly, could we help to renew the Dominican vision by taking more seriously the Order's commitment to study? Women have something unique to offer in their teaching and preaching as a result of their own reflective pondering on the word of God and their own penetrative interaction with theological truths. We are made aware of this by Catherine of Siena whose pondering produced a 'lived theology' which to this day is relevant and attractive. A lived theology is the fruit of prayer, study and a whole contemplative way of life. Jordan of Saxony, Dominic's successor, states that Dominic had the ability to pierce through to the hidden core of the many difficult questions of his day, 'thanks to a humble intelligence of the heart.'[11] A humble intelligence of the heart, such as Dominic and Catherine had, is both a necessary requirement, and a result, of the kind of study to which we are called as Dominicans. It is open to all of us. The Acts of the last General Chapter of the Order remind us that study seen and undertaken in this spirit unfolds itself as 'intellectual compassion'.[12] Intellectual compassion allows us to share the 'mercy of truth' (*misericordia veritatis*) with others in our preaching. Can we regard study in this light?

All these questions are not just vague, rhetorical or speculative. Rather they have a direct relevance to our daily prayer, to our relationships, to our ministry, to the manner in which we deal with suffering, to the way we watch the evening news, to the thoughts and feelings we have as we look at the moon on a cloudless night, to the plans and hopes we have for the coming years, and certainly to the invitation before us to renew the Dominican vision. And there are many other questions we can put to one another.

In preparing this talk, I have had the joy of reading through the Acts and Reports of recent General Chapters in our various congregations, and I have been impressed by the depth and breadth of our dreams and hopes for our world and for our Church recorded in them. Let us not forget these dreams and hopes. They have the ability to ignite our Dominican passion of possibility.

CONCLUSION

On 15 August 1217, Dominic gathered his small band of followers in Prouilhe around a statue of Mary, and then sent them out in all directions to spread the good news of God's love and truth. Some were willing to go; others were hesitant or afraid, but Dominic with his eyes burning brightly believed in the divine possibilities within them. 'Hoarded grain rots,' he had told them. To each he said: 'Go in trust. The Lord will be with you. You will lack for nothing.' Not all were confident of success; possibly not all even believed the time was ripe for dispersal. But they went. And in their going they discovered possibilities way beyond their wildest dreams.

Likewise, when Mary Lynch and Julian Nolan heard the call to bring Dominican religious life for women back to Ireland from Spain in 1686, Julian who was actually 75 years old and Mary Lynch who was in her 60s, could easily have refused. Can you imagine all the reasons they could have had for not going? 'We're too old.' 'My arthritis is crippling me.' 'I've a bad heart.' 'We'll get nobody to join us.' 'We'd do more good by spending our remaining days quietly here.' But, as we know, that's not how the story goes. Our story tells us of two brave women whose eyes were burning with the longing to see a new possibility, the possibility of Dominican women living, praying, teaching, serving others once again in this country. Because of their passion of possibility, we are all here.

Finally, the basic question, which we all have to ask ourselves, is whether our idea of the possible is too small. Has what is possible lost its elasticity and expansiveness, its power to surprise? Have we forgotten that, as Thomas Aquinas reminds us, the universe is fashioned 'after God's own heart ', and that God for whom 'all things are possible' wants this universe to reach its greatest potential? Is it that we have ruled out from our thinking, and even from our faith-life, the truth that within us, and among us, the Holy Spirit is groaning, longing to bring creation to its fulfilment, its infinite possibility in God? (Rom 8:22-7)

Questions such as these must surely take us into prayer, into a contemplative, receptive stance before God, the One who makes possible what seems impossible. In the account of the Transfiguration given in Mark's Gospel, we read that Jesus took the three disciples with him up a high mountain where they could be alone by themselves and witness his transformation. The high mountain is sometimes seen as a symbol of the contemplative journey the disciples had to make before they were able to see Jesus with new eyes. On our contemplative mountain, we are given new eyes, God's eyes. In this sacred place we may best discover fresh ways of fanning into flame the fire of passion for the possible.

Can you hold your passion of possibility lovingly, asking it to stretch you and bring you to new places and situations where God's message of love and compassion needs to be heard? Can I? Can you open yourself to the contemplative yearnings of your heart, and let them bring you to new depths of relationship with God? Can I? Can you and I live in a new way the motto of our Order: 'to contemplate and to pass on to others the fruit of our contemplation'? If we can even hesitantly stammer a 'Yes' to these questions, because of our belief not in ourselves, but in God's grace working within and among us, we will be doing our part in the renewal of the Dominican vision, for the sake of the coming of the reign of God in our world.

RESPONSE

The Gift of Remembering
Our Valiant Women
Congregation of St Mary, New Orleans, USA

MARY EDMUND GIBSON, O.P. *and*
MARY C. DANIEL, O.P.

During the early days of the Symposium, *From Threads to Tapestry*, we were reminded that in remembering the valiant women who founded our Congregations we were in touch with the maps of our personal and collective identities. If we merely repeat the stories, we lose the golden thread of our histories. We are invited to draw strength from these memories and in the presence and power or the Holy Spirit, to discern how we are called to expend our strength as Women of the Order of Preachers in this twenty-first Century. In the context of this background we remember some of our sisters of both the past and the present who expended their strength for the sake of the Word.

The Lord sent them out two by two, as did our Father Dominic. However, in the year 1860, 'seven valiant women' were sent forth from Ireland to the United States, to the city of New Orleans in Louisiana.

Rev. Jeremiah Moynihan, Pastor of St John the Baptist Church, needed sisters to teach the children his parish. He ventured forth to Cabra and requested sisters to staff St John's Parochial School. On October 9, 1860, the seven valiant women set sail for New Orleans. The vessel docked on November 5, 1860, and these missionaries planted their feet firmly on the ground in their new home and began their ministry of Catholic Education, a ministry still sponsored by the St Mary's Dominicans one hundred-forty-three years later.

Who were these seven valiant women? Mother Mary John Flanagan, thirty-three years of age, whose family motto was: 'Fortune Favours the Bold.' Mother Mary John lived this motto in a radical way. Her fortune was her boldness, and this is borne out in her leadership of the small and courageous band of Dominican missionaries. However, the history and tradition of St. Mary's, New Orleans, is the story of all seven sisters.

Mother Mary Magdalen O'Farrell, thirty-eight years of age and assistant prioress, began the New Orleans Female Dominican Academy in 1861. Today that institution is a thriving secondary school for girls with approximately one thousand students. Sister Mary Hyacinth McQuillan, twenty-one years old, assisted Sister Mary Magdalen in the Academy. The students called her 'the beautiful nun.' She died at the age of twenty-eight. Sisters Mary Osanna Cahill, thirty-five, and Bridget Smith, thirty-one, were lay sisters who did the manual labour while the other sisters taught. They were loved by the students, because they gave out apples and cookies during recess. Sister Mary Xavier Gaynor, twenty-four, was a novice who received the habit before leaving for New Orleans. She began the first circulating library in Louisiana. Sister Mary Ursula O'Reilly left the Congregation when times were bitterly difficult.

When the Civil War broke out in the United States several months after the arrival of the sisters, the Cabra Motherhouse invited them to return home, but these bold women were made of tougher stuff. They were no strangers to hardship and daily struggles.

Yet another hardship took the form of several yellow fever epidemics, which decimated the population of the city. Perhaps, the most difficult of many challenges was the fact that the sisters' property at St. John's had to be auctioned owing to the mismanagement of funds by the pastor. The sisters, with characteristic boldness and fidelity, went from door to door begging for funds. Eventually they were able to buy their property back.

In 1910, St. Mary's Dominican College was born, when the State of Louisiana authorized our Academy to confer degrees and diplomas, appertaining to letters and arts known to the universities and colleges of Europe and America. The college was blessed with seventy-five years of life. Its story can be boldly told. It was the first Catholic College for women in a five-state area.

During these one hundred forty three years, St. Mary's Dominican Sisters have been leaders in the ministry of preaching the Word in New Orleans with the characteristic boldness of our founders - valiant women proclaiming the Word.

Evidence of this boldness can be seen today in our fostering of the Dominican Alliance and Dominican Cluster. Sister Thérèse Leckert, from St Mary's, New Orleans, was instrumental in the founding of these two entities, which call us beyond ourselves to explore how Congregations of different historic origin can come together as Congregations of Dominican Women to more effectively preach the Word. The Alliance, with ten Congregations, focuses on ways of collaboration in our ministries, retreats, and study days, while retaining our particular identities. The Cluster, whose constitutive Congregations form the Alliance, focuses on actual re-configuration of these Congregations. There are currently four Congregations in the Cluster, with an additional four contemplating joining the group. The future of these two groups is not yet clear, and supporting these endeavours requires a certain boldness of spirit as we press forward into an unknown future. That is our call and we accept it in the same spirit as did our founders when they left Cabra in Ireland bound for New Orleans.

As Père Lacordaire has said: 'Tradition is an essential element in the life of any creature that lives in time. It is not only the memory of things which are no more; it is the continuity of the past into the future.'

RESPONSE

Unimaginable Journeys
Dominican Sisters of Eastern Australia and the Solomon Islands

ROSEMARY LEWINS, O.P. *and*
ELIZABETH HELLWIG, O.P.

As far back as our Sisters [1] can remember, and up until the 1880s, September was characterised by significant reading in the refectory. First, presumably since about 1913, the exploits of Mrs Bellew's family and the hundred years at Channel Row were told us through the *Cabra Annals* – that amazing foundation myth, whatever its historical selectivity.[2]

And second, the events of our own pioneering beginnings on 10th September 1867, were told briefly from the few pages of the original *Maitland Annals*. Then in 1958, our first Sister to visit our 'mother-house' at Dun Laoghaire, Sister Mary Norbert Hall, was given to bring home that hallowed gift – the account of the voyage to Australia on the *Martha Birnie* in 1867. This fascinating, humorous, detailed and free-spirited description of a horrendous journey of eighty-one days on the high seas, aboard a tiny sailing ship, introduced us to Mother Mary Agnes Bourke and our other pioneer Sisters, and the sacrifices they had made, their sense of adventure, and the depth of their commitment to Catholic education, in a way that nothing else could.

Travelling by sailing ship was not for the fainthearted. Even in the late 1880s, one in ten British sailing ships was lost at sea, and one in twenty crewmen lost his life. There exist only about 850 diaries of this period, and just 14% of these are by women. About 400,000 Irish emigrants arrived in Australia during the nineteenth century, but only a handful of Irish diaries were found. We have two, so we are blessed indeed.

That first journey and the details of the other five voyages undertaken by the thirty-five young women who were to become the backbone of our young Congregation, would transpose into a great film! Susan Sarandon would make a wonderful Mother Mary Agnes, and Nicole Kidman could perhaps take the role of Catherine Coghlan, the young novice whose sister, Margaret, an aspirant, died on the voyage and was buried in the deep. Then there is Father Stone, a difficult priest-companion to whom Tom Cruise might do justice! The film would begin with the awful leave-taking, on Kingstown pier, that literal launching out into the deep and letting go – and letting God.

The setting would provide total lack of privacy, eight women in one cabin for eighty-one days, no opportunity for baths, which, although paid for, were on the men's side of the ship; impossible canvas bunks to sleep on; a cockroach plague; music and Italian lessons, and religious instruction for children on board; friendly priests and seamen – and some not overdoing it; the kind doctor who declares that women's brains are smaller than men's and the sisters' mirthful response. There are individual episodes of grief at the partings; fear of the terrible seas at times; a shipwreck; Mass up to three times a day when the weather is fine, and weekly Confession in the saloon; learning signing by moonlight from a deaf steerage passenger; playing dominos, making rosary beads; hours and hours of sitting on deck, sometimes hanging on for dear life; a stowaway; exchange of recipes with the black cook from Barbados; wondering how everyone is doing back in Ireland; confidence in the prayers of their sisters for their safety; disappointment at first sight of the Southern Cross; displays of relics, black dresses, trunks, suntans, concussion, soakings, unrelenting seasickness, stray pigs, shark-sightings, sea birds, porpoises, passing ships, copious quantities of champagne – that wonderful stomach settler ...

By the time they arrived in Sydney, the Sisters loved the new land – just for being there! These cultured, well-educated women knew each other well by the end of the voyage, and each one was different on arrival from the person who had set foot on the boat in dear old Ireland. In 1867, Archdeacon MacEncroe reportedly told Bishop Murray, with tears in his eyes, that 'a finer batch of nuns has never come to the colony'.

The statistics reveal an amazing picture. Between 1867 and 1888, thirty-five young women connected with St Mary's Kingstown / Dun Laoghaire volunteered to come to the other side of the world, knowing that they could never return home. Only thirteen of them had been professed more than one year. Eighteen of them were under twenty-five. It is all there – that single-mindedness, that 'holy naiveté', for the sake of the Gospel – in the tradition of those earlier 'Founders', Juliana Nolan and Mary Lynch, who had returned from long exile in Spain to re-found a convent of Dominican women in Galway in 1686; their sisters of Channel Row, Dublin in 1717, and the risk-takers of Cabra in the 1860s – that strong sense of mission, of 'up she gets, for up she must!' regardless of personal cost, and with perhaps a sniff of a sense of adventure! [3] They were full-bodied, warm-blooded women who were faced with hard work, totally alien conditions and wild colonial children. Unlike other migrants to Australia, who came to make a better life for themselves, our sisters were ready to provide a better life for others. They had no concept of their future, but they never doubted that they had one. They had confidence in their own ability to make a difference, at the frontier, where no one else was available to undertake the challenge. They not only believed to their bones in education for women, but were to provide it with an incredibly high level of excellence. They took their place, alongside their bishop, in the midst of an impoverished Irish colonial church, greatly enriching it with their presence.

The wells that hold their memory are well tended. These

women now have their place in the general pioneering history of Australian women. The 1867 diary was published, and recently the national broadcaster made two programmes around it. On the 135th anniversary of their arrival a plaque was placed in the courtyard of St Patrick's Church in Sydney, where they went to give thanks for the journey and ask for blessings on the new venture. Their names also have a place on the 'Welcome Wall' at the Australian Maritime Museum, along with the ancestors of other migrant families who settled the Australia we know today. Their Anniversaries and Professions are noted in our Congregation's daily journal, *Journey*, along with the significant people and events in our wider Dominican story. There have been re-enactments of our older community foundations, and we treasure our plots in the general cemeteries around the country as sacred places for re-membering. We continue to be proud of and humbled by their courage, their commitment and their passion for the sharing of their faith. We *will* remember them, and know that they in turn intercede on our behalf.

In 1897, the sister of our first Australian Prioress General, Mother Mary Joseph de Lauret, arrived home from abroad with a sapling from St Dominic's orange tree in Rome. It still grows proudly at Santa Sabina, Strathfield, New South Wales, and bears abundant fruit, a constant reminder of perhaps the most precious gift that our Irish sisters left with us – the Dominican charism.

By 1890, there were twenty-three Irish Sisters and thirty-one Australian born Sisters in our congregation, and the average age was twenty-seven! Thirty-four of their ex-students had entered other fledgling religious groups, and twenty-two had entered the novitiate in Maitland. By 1900, they had already set up four significant branch houses, and undertaken a ministry to deaf children. Fr. Bede Jarrett, O.P., at this time was worrying about finding the money to build a priory at Oxford. Yet our women had built five large convents and schools in colonial

Australia.

On the shoulders of the early Irish sisters' outstanding business acumen and reputation for sound and broad education, the Australian Dominicans were able to offer secondary education for girls thirty or forty years before the government schools were set up in the same country areas. Certainly, the schools were limited by the thinking and mores of the time, but as the early twentieth century brought more foundations, the sisters continued to provide an education system that was widely recognised for its focus on quality, excellence and culture.

Mary McAleese, President of Ireland, visiting Sydney in March 2003, shared her appreciation of her own Dominican education in St Dominic's High School, Belfast, and noted the wonderful role-modelling of independence and individuality which she gained from the Sisters. These traits, which we believe our sisters too tried to foster, attracted young Australian women to the Order and encouraged many of our students to pursue university education and thus to contribute to law, medicine, politics and many other professional fields in Australia.

In the mid-twentieth century, our congregation's focus continued to be entirely on education. However, the story was not all expansion, success and educational accolades. The sisters, parents and students lived through influenza epidemics, massive world depression, two world wars, and a highly structured, sometimes deprived life. We remember here too that small but vital group of women – our lay sisters who supported and often humanised the educational ministry.

Vatican II and the consequent changes in the church brought some pain and confusion. Wonderful sisters left; others fell into depression. Most relished new initiatives in community life and in education, and some, to others' consternation, explored new ministries.

In 1956, the four Dominican congregations in Australia, in partnership with the Dominican friars made a pioneering foundation in the Western Solomon Islands. At the time 'the happy isles' were a subsistence economy of people living in interdependent villages whose only method of transport was by canoe. The Solomonese people were grateful for the missionary presence and together, people and missionaries, enthusiastically built schools and churches and clinics.

Like their Irish forebears, these valiant Dominican men and women lived lives unimaginable to contemporary Australian Dominicans: no hot water, no electricity – except occasionally from temperamental generators – no phones, an irregular postal service, and immense isolation. With great confidence, postulants were accepted and today the twenty-three professed sisters and two novices form Holy Rosary Vicariate of the Dominican Sisters of Eastern Australia and the Solomon Islands.

However, the future for these sisters is not clear. The Solomon Islands economy has collapsed, the government is corrupt, the police force has no power, and schools and colleges have been forced to close. The sisters, and therefore our whole Congregation, are faced with constant challenges – for formation, education and survival.

So where is our Congregation now, after one hundred and thirty six years of ministry and presence in Australia? Our one hundred and fifty three sister descendents of those early Irish pioneer Dominicans now can be found in six states of Australia in primary, secondary, tertiary and special education settings, in administration and research, in country and city parish ministry, in RCIA, in ecumenics, hospital, university and prison chaplaincy, in nursing and family-planning clinics, in retreat centres and spiritual direction, in pastoral care, counselling and welfare, working among aboriginal and migrant communities, with the materially poor, and those with physical or intellectual handicap, drug and alcohol dependency and AIDS, with the homeless, with those in prison and their children, with asylum seekers and refugees.

We value our partnership with our Associates, Dominican Friars, Dominican lay men and women through membership of the Dominican Family. Together with three other congregations of Dominican women, we form the Federation of Dominican Sisters of Australia, and we rejoice in being foundation members of Dominican Sisters International.

We continue to discern and articulate our charism as Australian Dominican women. In the words of Joan Chittister O.S.B., we are conscious that

> we need to stand up together, to link arms with the great ones of the past, in order to find within ourselves the Great Heart it will take to shape the future... May all the Sisters who have walked before us lead us together into the mind of God. Then, together, may we find a passion for life and become ourselves, for the next generation, fragments of the face of God.[4]

.

A Tapestry Explored
Domincian Sisters of South Australia

ANGELA MOLONEY, O.P.

I was born in Meath St, Dublin (1937), the second of, eventually, eight children born to Agnes and William. I lived the first six years of my life in the city. After First Holy Communion at St Joseph's National School, Stoneybatter, my family moved to Cabra West.

My mother was creative and resourceful: a seamstress, chef, gardener, interior-decorator, midwife and much more. My father a singer, a storyteller, a bit of a poet, a hard worker, a deeply spiritual man ... a true Celt. Despite being poor, with the worry and stress of unemployment from time to time, we had a loving and nurturing home and a supportive extended family.

At the age of six-and-a-half, I transferred to 'the old school' run by the Dominican Sisters at Cabra, which seemed to metamorphose overnight into St Catherine's National School. Here I knew many of the Sisters, and was taught by Sisters Mary Bernard, Mary St John, Mary de Sales and the person who most augmented the good work of my parents, Sister Maureen Flanagan.

What wells of memory Maureen gave her class. For me, these wells have been visited with joy down the years, and deepened. Not because I gained literacy skills (I was to discover in later years that dyslexia is endemic in my family), but because Maureen related to us in a way that gave us a sense of our dignity and worth. She gave working-class kids a thirst for education and the bigger meanings in life, and led us into wonderful and magical worlds where these meanings could be tasted – the worlds of music, poetry and story. We learnt to read the *sol-fah*, and to sing Gregorian Chant, motets by Palestrina, Moore's melodies, *agus amhráin Gaeilge*. Here we met Shakespeare, Moore, Yeats, Wordsworth, John Henry Newman, Handel, Bach and many others. These sources of enrichment, joy and hope leave us deeply grateful to Sister Maureen.

With a flick of the wrist, so to speak, let us turn now to South Australia's panel in the 'tapestry'.[1]

The panel created to 'represent' something of our Congregation's life and context shows South Australia's coastline and territory. The red and black Sturt Pea, which grows profusely in the desert, is our floral emblem. With the Aboriginal flag, which symbolises the red earth, the black people and the bright sun, we acknowledge the Indigenous people of Australia, and acknowledge too that we reside on their lands. The Adelaide Plains are the home of the Kaurna People. In recent years, as we acknowledge the cultural and ecological devastation wrought by the coming of white people to Australia, and journey slowly with our Indigenous sisters and brothers towards healing, Kaurna Elders have graciously welcomed us to their land.

Then we honour Mother Teresa Moore and her pioneering companions. Oak leaves and acorns represent the seeds of Dominican life that they brought from a cool green Ireland to a beautiful but strange, 'sunburnt country'. Theirs was a painful and troubled history in a struggling new colony and in a young and confused Church, riven with internal political strife and power struggles; political strife in which our Sisters were 'more sinned against that sinning.' Indeed our annals record that our early history was 'too sad to be told in full'. And so it was not told in an honouring way for over a century.[2]

It was not until after we had grown into a feminist consciousness in the 1980s that, in 1993, we created and enacted a ritual-pilgrimage around the historic campus of St Mary's, Franklin Street, in Adelaide. This place of our early history is seen in the second picture on our panel. It shows the historic chapel (where

Blessed Mary McKillop[3] was excommunicated) and the convent. St Mary's continues to be a primary and secondary girls' college with a fine reputation.

In this emotive ritual we honoured our pioneer Sisters, we lamented their suffering and we celebrated the 'tree of Dominican life' that they had planted. This tree, which eventually grew strong, became Australian and flourished in the Australian context with strong roots in the soil of their vision and painful labour. We were gladdened and healed by this experience and now we celebrate foundation day each year on December 5th. And I felt that our pioneer Sisters were also healed and gladdened by our awakening to and embracing, at last, their story with its suffering, sadness and struggle, and by our reclaiming their good names and their generous and vulnerable humanity.

The third picture is of Cabra Convent, the boarding house built 'in the country' less than twenty years (1886) after the arrival of the first seven sisters. Cabra, now only ten minutes drive south of Adelaide, is a thriving, co-ed middle and senior school of over one thousand students. Residences for our retired Sisters are on land adjacent to the College. In the last ten years or so we have reclaimed our chapel space (a small basilica built on the same plan as Cabra, Dublin) for a Cabra Chapel Community. This Community prepares and celebrates a participative and inclusive Eucharist on Sundays. It gives me hope to see people thus reclaiming their baptismal priesthood. Indeed, when, on occasion, there is no ordained person to preside, while we lament the Eucharistic famine so unnecessarily prevalent in our Church, this liturgy is nourishing and empowering and foreshadows with confidence a new way of being Church. For many of us, Cabra Chapel Eucharist is our life-line and it keeps us connected to the institutional Church.

The eucalyptus tree symbolises the blossoming and fruitfulness of the many and diverse ministries down the decades of all the sisters who belonged to our Holy Cross community. It includes ministries to the hearing-impaired and to children with various disabilities, and ministry in the Solomon Islands. It includes those who stayed with us through all our transformations in lifestyle, theologies and understandings of power ... and those who gave rich years of creative ministry and eventually left us for other life choices, carrying the Dominican ethos into the rest of their life. Happily, most of these women remain our very good friends. While celebrating many valiant women of former times, I also want to honour some courageous Dominican women, brilliant educators who sparked creativity in an era (1945-60) when, sadly, rigorous study and intellectual pursuits were feared by persons in authority. These great women, among them Thérèse Sweeney and Kate Horgan (both of whom died in the last few weeks), re-ignited Dominican spirituality in my generation. They enkindled anew the fires of creativity, wonder and joy in the search for truth and beauty. They fired the imagination of both their students and the young Sisters whom they trained to be Dominican educators. This they did at personal cost in a context of mistrust and disapproval. Their persistent efforts have given many of us vision and joyful hope even until now.

Further, I want to honour the memory of all the women who suffered because a hierarchical, 'power-over' model was falsely 'sanctified'. I give thanks that we have grown to know that shared power is sacred power, Christic power. Sharing this divine power, we are co-creators with Sophia-God, one day at a time.

As our community ages, the numbers in active ministries grow fewer; yet these ministries are diverse. They range from justice and peace representative in the Asia-Pacific Region to industrial counsellor, lecturer in theology and biblical studies at tertiary level, founder and director of a centre for sexually and physically abused children, deputy principal of St Dominic's Priory (the English Dominican foundation in Adelaide), coordinator of Sophia, our Christian Feminist Spirituality centre. Finally, our panel shows *Sophia*. *Sophia* is a purpose-built Christian feminist centre, a corporate expression of our commitment to a feminist perspective in all of our ministries. It too, is situated in our Cabra grounds and is twelve years old. *Sophia* is a profoundly ecumenical place on the margins of the Churches. And while several of our sisters work there, it is increasingly dependent on a growing number of skilled and committed women volunteers. They desire to help *Sophia* continue into the future as a sacred space for women where the struggle for justice for all people and our earth can continue.[3]

The Celtic cross on our 'tapestry' honours the memory of our deceased sisters. Each grave is marked with a simple Celtic cross.[4]

Although we have in recent years, because of aging and fewer Sisters, closed convents and handed over colleges and parish primary schools, the Dominican ethos has been sought after by the principals and staff of these schools, and is perhaps more boldly proclaimed than in the past. Dominican Sisters sit on school councils and boards of management. So the tree of ministries within a Dominican ethos continues to grow and to influence the young people educated in Dominican schools, now fully-staffed by lay teachers. Something Australian has grown, taking vision and hope into the future!

RESPONSE

'To Do for God What the Miners Do for Gold'

Domincian Sisters of Aotearoa-New Zealand, 1871-2003

CARMEL WALSH, O.P.

Our Dominican foundresses came into a very European and colonising environment; they were making history, not remembering it. It was in October 1870, that ten women, some of the most able of the Sion Hill community, set out from Ireland: [1]

> Mother Gabriel Gill, ages 33 – the prioress of the new community; a woman of strong courage and indomitable courage; Sister Agnes Rooney, aged 59 – the sub-prioress; a beautiful pianist, singer, linguist, historian; Sister Francis Sullivan, aged 37 – a skilled linguist and a great teacher, excellent in history and botany; Sister Vincent Whitty, aged 37 – a gentle woman, she took charge of the infant classes at the parish school; Sister Catherine Hughes, aged 40 – the first appointed Mistress of Schools, a splendid organiser as well as a highly gifted musician and a lover of literature; Sister Gertrude Dooley, aged 33 – in charge of the parish school, the artist *par excellence* of the community; Sister de Ricci Kirby, aged 33 – appointed Mistress of Novices; Sister Bertrand McLaughlin, aged 19 – the youngest of the group, who was to spend 76 years in New Zealand; Sister Lucy Tracy, professed 12 years – a lay sister who had lived for several years in Paris and had an easy command of French; Sister Peter Jordan, aged 21 – a lay sister, professed two days after she had been chosen for the new mission.

After a long and sometimes dangerous journey the Sisters arrived in Dunedin on the 18 February 1871. Two days after their arrival they took charge of the Catholic girls' school in Dunedin; within a week they opened a high school for day pupils. A great educational tradition was begun.

These were deeply contemplative women, rooted in their Dominican tradition and customs, highly educated and imbued with a strong sense of mission. They had among them the political, economic and leadership skills crucial for the success of their educational work. Their aim was to implant and recreate in New Zealand the institutional lifestyle they had lived in Ireland. This was possible in the towns where schools and boarding schools were established.

At the same time the sisters were called to respond to the need of the impoverished Irish immigrants, by providing them with a Catholic environment and faith instruction. In time, many sisters lived among the people often in isolated areas in small convents of three or four – far removed from what had been their experience in Ireland.

As far as possible they maintained the monastic tradition in which they had been trained but practical realities mitigated their degree of 'apartness' from ordinary society. In many and often hidden ways, the sisters shared the hardships and poverty experienced by those to whom they ministered, supporting themselves by what they could earn, as well as by the generosity of those who shared goods with them. These early sisters saw their mission as chiefly with the Irish immigrants, the settler Church, not the *Tangata Whenua* – the Maori people. Mother Gabriel Gill's injunction to Sisters in both Australia and New Zealand sums up her missionary vision: 'Are you prepared to do for God what the miners do for gold?'

We came to a new understanding of these amazing yet ordinary women, not just as Foundresses but as true missionaries, after 1984, when New Zealand sisters first read the home letters of their Foundresses in the archives at Sion Hill Convent, Dublin, and we realised that we possessed only one side of our story, one of fact and accomplishment. The human side had come through rarely, sometimes in letters to bishops and once on a death certificate which read 'Cause of Death: Exhaustion.' The *history* was recorded in New Zealand but the *story* lay hidden in those envelopes in Dublin – a story that was woven out of the letters of the first Sisters to their friends in Sion Hill. Mother Gabriel Gill, Sisters Francis Sullivan and Louis Keighron wrote in detail to Ireland, and Sister de Ricci Kirby wrote frequently and at length to her uncle, Dr Kirby, Rector of the Irish College in Rome.

The contents of these letters are precious to us now, for they contain memoirs which can energise the present-day reader to responses of admiration, gratitude, mirth (sometimes) and even incredulity.

For a memoir is more than an act of remembering, but a narrative that encapsulates an individual's life experience *and* passes on to the reader something of the author's attitude. In the Sion Hill letters we have come to know some of our Foundresses in a new way. Now we see them as truly human beings, living and breathing with feeling, emotion and even prejudice, just like us!

It is only during the past fifteen years or so that, as individuals and as a Congregation, we have become aware and publicly proud of our early Sisters. This development parallels a similar movement in our society, where genealogical societies have grown up, and micro-histories of individuals, communities and their activities, relationships and values arouse interest and admiration.

The Sisters did not write reminiscences for the 'future historian' as many of the early settlers did. They were very aware of how their leader and bishop regarded their role in the diocese. He called them his 'auxiliaries in establishing civilising influences among his flock.' This was a noble description in 1871, and Bishop Moran when he worked in Grahamstown in South Africa had tested the worth of the Dominicans there. So the Sisters were reluctant to write detailed records for New Zealand, unlike Moran, who founded a weekly Catholic newspaper, *The Tablet*, which became a powerful shaper of conscience and public opinion in the Irish Catholic community throughout the whole country. The early Sisters were very polite in what they recorded in New Zealand. But what were their impressions of their new home, Dunedin – the 'Edinburgh of the South', and its people?

Mark Twain said of Dunedin: 'The people are Scotch. They stopped here on their way to heaven – thinking they had arrived.' [2]

Sister Francis Sullivan was none too impressed with the view from their house on the hill. She wrote:

> All the houses around are perched on the top of the hills, and to some of these there seems no entrance but by means of ladders. It is quite clear the people count on always having the use of their limbs or have resigned themselves to perpetual imprisonment should they lose them. No vehicle of any kind could get near any of the hall doors ...
>
> You never knew such a queer place as this and such queer people. [3]

Then the state of religion was a cause for concern:

> As to religion it is at the very lowest. You would be frightened in speaking to the children, that is even the very best brought up, they have no idea of it, even the name of God seems a strange sound to them, and what is worse, they seem to take so little interest in such topics, in fact it is almost impossible to interest them at all. Whilst in worldly matters they are more clever and wide awake than the old people at home. [4]

The children were not exactly impressive either:

> I fear we shall work hard before we make any impression on them. They are totally devoid of the bump of sensation, and as to being one bit more impressed by Bishops, Priests or Nuns, they are quite innocent of it. The smallest youth in the school seems to consider himself as good and great a man as the Pope.[5]

Conditions in colonial Dunedin evoked strong reactions. The Sisters faced new experiences of egalitarian attitudes, particularly among the socially inferior Irish immigrants. Few families kept servants because wages were high; mothers and children did most of the work and even the fathers took turns at minding the baby. Several letters recall such innovative ideas. Sister Mary Francis spoke volumes when she wrote:

> We have met some very good kind people, all dress very well, quite in fashion, but I don't believe we have seen a lady in the general acceptation of the word since we came here. Indeed I suspect there is scarcely one in the Colony.[6]

Sister De Ricci wrote bluntly to her uncle in Rome:

> You can have no idea of the difficulty of getting on with a class of people such as these are in Dunedin ... the low ignorant minds with which we have to deal. The catholic body here seems to be the dregs of society.[7]

Real ladies might have been in short supply, the children excessively worldly, but the state of the faith caused the early sisters gravest concern. Their missionary vision was seriously challenged. It was a long journey from Ireland to eternity, but subsequent correspondence replaces the homesickness and disillusionment of the exile with the pragmatism of the missionary and the educationalist.

After nine years, Mother Gabriel wrote home:

> I fear our Schools will not be commenced for some years ... We want money and nuns only to accomplish real missionary work on a gigantic scale. Ignorance and infidelity seem to poor [sic] into this dear land, and to increase as rapidly as the population. [8]

However the sisters did not give up. The building of convents and schools went ahead, with funds raised at bazaars, art unions and loans from Ireland. It took only seven years to move from the first borrowed convent to St Dominic's Priory, Dunedin, and send home letters on an engraved letterhead. Debt was something both the bishop and the Sisters feared, but there was a further insidious problem. Exhaustion from overwork and sparse living conditions in a rigorous climate encouraged tuberculosis. Novices, in particular, were susceptible. Only from the letters home can we glean something of the despondency surrounding the convents in the wake of constant terminal illness, increasing debt and the call to maintain standards and staffing levels in both the parochial schools and their own high schools.

At a recent Chapter this kind of information led us to new ways of reflecting on those who have gone before us.

In 1902, Sister Louis Keighron came to New Zealand specifically to help with teacher training for the Sisters. This was the time when the number of colonial-born equalled the number of Irish-born Sisters. Until the 1880s, a marked number of local postulants had come through the free parish schools and chosen to be professed as lay sisters. As such they presented no threat to the underlying power structures within the community. With the arrival of increased numbers of colonial aspirants with higher educational qualifications the scene began to change, for education held influence within community life in New Zealand as had been the case in Ireland. Sister Louis Keighron reported:

No doubt about it, Mother, the future of our Order in the Colonies, spiritual and temporal, depends on our home-trained Irish Sisters. The Colonials are excellent in many ways but I should never like to see them predominate in the Community.[9]

Thirty years later the issue surfaced again. In 1933, all rejoiced when the eagerly awaited transcript arrived, forming all the New Zealand houses into one Congregation. But the first Prioress General strongly exhorted the Sisters to suppress in the Dominican family anything approaching nationalism. Expressions such as 'the home Sisters', 'the New Zealanders', and 'the Irish Sisters' were viewed as being destructive of the unity called for in the Rule of St Augustine.[10] Needless comparisons and foolish boasting were to cease:

We should remember that once professed in the Order we are one family ... Patriotism is a virtue, Nationalism a vice, and one that thinking minds strongly denounce at the present day.[11]

These last examples invite special reflection for us today as they provide instances where the shadow side is acknowledged and a healing of our history has evolved over time. Healing of memory forms a large portion of the analytic framework of New Zealand history-writing in recent times. Today this issue is expressed in the justice issues of bi-culturalism, *Maori/Pakeha*.

The transition asked for by Vatican II was made possible by the foresight of the Congregation's leadership, by a determination to accept the opportunities for change offered by the Council – and by the strong-minded individual sisters who responded to the challenges put before them. These were women of strength and initiative; following in the footsteps of the early Sisters, they showed again that independence of spirit, that integrity based on the critical thinking in which they had been trained, that willingness to step out again on new paths, to walk a new way. There began an often painful reassessment of our whole way of life and many old established customs did not survive the process. During this time, Sisters became involved in areas of mission other than that solely based in the school – adult education, pastoral care of the deaf, areas of spirituality, social justice, chaplaincies, parish work. The sisters were claiming their place as religious and as women. This was often in an atmosphere of non-understanding on the part of some of the clergy and laity. Changes were at times misinterpreted and treated with suspicion.

As the social concerns of our time become so paramount – the needs of women and children, areas of justice, bi-culturalism, environment concerns – as issues of power, gender and religion are played out again and again, there are sisters in the forefront working both within and outside Church structures and in the ecumenical field. The sisters are striving to speak the truth when confronted with injustices, to challenge existing structures and to transform these when necessary, to heal areas of past woundedness, to empower others – especially women – by supporting, affirming and enabling them.

There is a new understanding of our internal ministry – the importance of the way we live and relate to one another, remaining alert to the issues of the time, the power of the pen, of prayer, as those more in the background give support and encouragement to the more active. The focus would seem to have moved from the role of the Sister to the person of the Sister, from performing tasks to witnessing as persons, and living in hope. We have identified five sources of strength and hope which we cherish as having been part of our heritage from our Foundresses:

- – our attentiveness to the 'signs of the times';
- – our love of education and learning;
- – our awareness of the needs of women;
- – our commitment to truth and justice;

– our foundation in prayer and preaching.

To conclude: in the Maori world, the normal way for finding out who we are, is to return home, to our land, to our people, and to be welcomed home into our own meeting house. In this way we can become one with the living and one with those who have died. We become part of the *whanau*, born again and renewed within the family. At this Jubilee Symposium we New Zealand Dominican Sisters find both old and new expression of that possibility: we rejoice and give thanks.

'Old Friends Are Best'

Domincian Sisters of Western Australia

REGINA O'NEILL, O.P.

Those of us who represent the Dominicans of Perth and Geraldton in Western Australia speak for all the Sisters beginning with Mother Gabriel Gill of Sion Hill, Dublin, and Dunedin, New Zealand, who have given their lives primarily to the teaching and the sharing of the faith in that far-flung part of the southern hemisphere.

The city of Perth is beautiful, but we are reminded often that it is, still, the most remote capital city in the world. That's a distinction nobody else can match.

In 1999, the Dominican Congregation of Western Australia celebrated the centenary of the arrival from Dunedin of Mother Gabriel Gill and companions. A brochure which was circulated for the centenary highlights the motto that led them all the way from beautiful Ireland and New Zealand to the harsh gold-mining towns of Western Australia; it is a motto which has carried us through the years also: 'To contemplate and to give to others the fruits of our contemplation'. Those Dominican women of a past age believed that their call was from God. Their ministry was the ministry of teaching.

Our centenary year, 1999, and all the celebrations that highlighted the Dominican presence in Western Australia for a century, brought the memory of Mother Gabriel Gill and our pioneer Sisters vividly before all of us. The pilgrimage many of us made to the outback places where the Sisters had lived and carried out their mission was a momentous occasion.

Especially memorable was the visit to the remote gold-mining town of Day Dawn where Mother Gabriel died alone in

1905. We could understand then the desolation of the little group left without a leader.

When, next day, we gathered at the original burial place in Cue where the Sisters had their little convent, and knelt at the spot thought to be the site of Mother Gabriel's grave in the public cemetery, we felt the wave of grief that must have overwhelmed those left mourning her.

The re-interment of Mother Gabriel and the remains of all the deceased Sisters in our part of the public cemetery at Perth, at the close of the centenary year, and the Mass celebrated there in the presence of all our Sisters and many ex-students and friends, was a moving experience. There was a feeling that all those who had gone before us had come home.

Now, I should like to revert to a personal memory. In 1950, Mother Laurence Prendiville came to Ireland, as many representatives of overseas congregations did, to interest girls in religious life overseas. She visited many schools, Dominican and otherwise, and spoke to many girls. Among those schools was Dominican College, Eccles Street, Dublin; and among the girls who listened to Mother Laurence in the same classroom at Eccles Street were Lucy Callaly and Nancy O'Neill. Lucy became Sister Mary Declan and I, became Sister M. Regina. Each of us was blessed with loving parents and brothers. That was, indeed, an age of faith; our parents, finally convinced that the call was a genuine call from God, agreed to allow their only daughters to enter a Dominican Congregation in a place called Dongara in Western Australia, and, in spite of, or, more accurately, through all the ups and downs of life, their faith in our calling was justified. If God had not decreed otherwise a few short weeks ago, Lucy Callaly, Sister M. Declan would have been here to speak for herself, but I am here instead to speak for both of us.[2] You will understand, then, how we Dominicans from Western Australia relate very specially to the theme of the last session of the conference: 'Designs on Hope: When Distance Becomes Communion'.

To be present at the symposium is an inspiration and a grace; an inspiration because we are enabled, again, to thank God for what has been, and a grace because under God it is the Irish Dominicans' gift to us. We know that everyone here is a friend, indeed an old friend with all the comfort that promises. I remember reading somewhere and I quote from an uncertain memory, 'Old friends are best.' King James (I don't know which one) used to call for his old shoes; they were easiest for his feet.

That's not the whole story, of course. We have always looked to Ireland and the Irish Dominicans as a source of inspiration, knowing that all of us belong to Dominic's Family, and – to mix the metaphor a little – each Congregation is a branch of the family tree. We can never be really independent of each other, nor do we wish to be. Our faith is in the One God who is Trinity and, under God, our faith is in the religious family to which we belong. May it be so today and tomorrow and all the tomorrows in God's calendar.

Here's a footnote that I can't resist. When Mother Laurence called on an Irish bishop or archbishop in 1950 (it could have been John Charles McQuaid of happy memory) he heard her out, and then put his question, the very last question she expected: 'If girls go with you to Western Australia, will they be well-fed?' She gave him an assurance that they would, and left him with the impression that they would be going to a land flowing with milk and honey. Actually, Mother Laurence gave the archbishop a good press. She thought his question was quite perspicacious, especially as she was able to put her hand on her heart and give a cast-iron guarantee that they would be well-fed. So, if Mother Laurence is listening in from above and Lucy, Sister Declan beside her, I want to say that the guarantee she gave was the genuine article: to use an Australianism, it was 'fair dinkum'.

In the novitiate at Dongara we were well-fed and well-cared

for. As young Dominicans, we learned to pray the Divine Office, and although our Latin was scanty we learned to love the great prayer of the Church. Mother Laurence was a fine educator. In her hierarchy of values, education was a priority; each one of us was expected to apply herself to the best of her ability to the work of education, both the ongoing education of self and the education of students of all ages entrusted to us.

A last word from the simple wisdom of an anonymous writer: 'Lord, thank you for showing me that with you there is no need for feelings of failure. For whatever I cannot do is left free to be completed by you in your time and your way.'

Therein lies our hope.

HOMILY
One More Loaf to Offer

MARGARET SCHARF, O.P.

The gospel today ends with the infamous phrase '... not including the women and children.' Suffice to say that I will be referring to the women and children later in this reflection!

I could reflect with you on the eucharistic sense of Jesus' action in this story; dwell on the fact that this act came after Jesus has heard the tragic news of the death of his cousin, John the Baptist; that here we have a story of the immense compassion of Jesus. However, as I reflected on this text something else struck me, and it is from the well of this reflection that I will share.

In this story, Jesus gives us a clear indication that something new and important is about to happen. He steps out of the boat and into people's lives. He steps out into the midst of the people. The crowd gathers around him, a community of listeners who feast on his every word. Then, he challenges this newly-founded community to continue the feeding. They come, are fed, and are missioned to feed others.

We immediately pick up that the disciples were hesitant at the task set before them, but Jesus as it were, insists: 'You already have a gift – feed them yourselves!'

Jesus took the five loaves and two fish, blessed and broke them in the traditional way, and shared them with those around him. I think that it was at this point that the women played their important part. It is hard to believe that all of those people gathered there did not have any food. Women would have been travelling from the market to families, or from families who offered food. Women can always produce food to feed a crowd

---

A homily preached on 4 August, 2003.
The readings were: Numbers 11:4-15 and Mark 14:13-21

without much warning.

Out from their *own* baskets came enough food for everybody and more. I believe that the miracle performed here was that people learned to share from their resources, that those present, and let us name them – the women present – got the message of what Jesus was doing in the midst of them, and did likewise, as only women can do. *This* is the way of the new community centred on Jesus. *This* is the way we are all called to be.

You may recall that one of the earliest pieces of Christian art is an ancient mosaic of the second century, depicting the loaves and fish. It is a well-known piece of art. But have you looked at it in detail? There are only four loaves and not five. Local tradition has it that the reason there are only four loaves is that *we* are challenged to add the fifth loaf. We are called to be bread for others.

We read in the Book of Numbers of God's gift of manna to the people in the desert, and I want to talk a little about the manna of our lives. What is the manna of today? God's manna has fallen upon us in a myriad of ways, some of which we have not even noticed. I would like to speak of two of those ways:

The first could be called God's *gift* to us, which comes in the following forms: The talents we have been given; the skills we have learned; our educational and artistic backgrounds; and even our own personalities, our ways of being, are gift for ourselves and others.

Then, we have the *givens* of our lives. God's manna has fallen in such ways as the very place where I find myself at any point in time, the spirituality of place. There are other givens over which I have little control, but which nevertheless, are gift: the family into which I was born, the culture in which I grew up, and the religious beliefs I hold to, based on the modelling of a faith community to which I belong. It is out of these *gifts* and *givens* that we are challenged by Jesus to feed others.

Valiant women give from the storehouse of gifts and givens,

even when it seems there is nothing more to give. Look around you at the women gathered here, today. We are all valiant women. We have all heard a call and responded from the storehouse of who we are as women, as Dominicans.

I would like to share a little story with you from the diary of Sister Mary de Pazzi, one of our founding sisters in Western Australia. Fortunately, she wrote a fine diary, outlining the exploits of the little band of sisters in the first year of their arrival at Greenough in 1899. One of the most poignant stories of this period describes the hardship of poverty the sisters had to constantly face. Many of the local people paid the sisters in kind for the tuition of their children, that is, gave the sisters meat, vegetables and fruit instead of money. De Pazzi made the comment one time, that this was all well and good, but food wasn't going to pay their bills!

At one point, the sisters had only two eggs left, and there was a little anxiety about this reality. Then the parish priest arrived back from his journeying to various places, having said Mass for the isolated communities. The priests' lives were not glamorous, either. They, too, struggled with the isolation and poverty of the region, and rode hundreds of miles on horseback to visit small communities, oftentimes, saying Mass in the homes of the farmers. De Pazzi wrote of taking the last two eggs, the last of their food, and having made a dish of scrambled eggs, giving it to the priest. He, of course, was delighted, and after eating went on his way again, leaving the sisters to ponder what they were to eat in their future. Just at that point, and to their great relief, a woman arrived at the back door with meat for the sisters! These valiant sisters gave from the only manna they had, out of their meagre storehouse of food and of courage to face the unknowns of their daily lives.

So, what about us? We listened to the grumbling of the Israelites not content with their manna, their gifts from God (Num 11:4-15). What we are all invited to do is not grumble about our gifts or givens, but to hand these over to nurture the community, the people of God. In doing so, the sharing becomes a transforming experience; in a sense, a real Eucharist. For, the Word in me becomes blessed and broken, an action to be done over and over, and to be remembered.

HOMILY
Transfiguration: What Rising from the Dead Might Mean

JUDITH LAWSON, O.P.

The account of the Transfiguration is such that, rather as in a patterned tapestry the threads of which weave and change in colour and tone, we are offered rich images to reflect upon as we seek to make meaning from the mystery.

Anne Thurston's reference to the Transfiguration in her presentation challenges us to imagine Miriam and Mary of Magdala present on Mount Tabor alongside Jesus and the three apostles, together too with other valiant women. I shall enjoy taking that imagining forward.

My own reflection on the Gospel began by pondering the reactions of the apostles to the experience: Peter's desire to hold on to the moment permanently – his reflection expressed many years later in his Letter which is our First Reading – and the connection it might offer us today as we take up the theme of contemplation and the call to mission.

All of us recall within our lives special moments of strong significance – moments that connect us to a deeper level of meaning, but which we find difficult to describe; moments we want to hold on to and treasure.

I recall a few such treasured moments that were part of my long journey here to this symposium: celebrating Eucharist with Irish Dominican sisters in the village of Jane of Aza, close to Caleruega; sitting facing the east window in the monastery of Iona with a group of pilgrims from around the world, praying

---

Homily for the Feast of the Transfiguration.
The readings were: 2 Peter 1: 16-19; Mark 9: 2-8

Morning Prayer; singing the *Salve* with the Dominican Sisters at Prouilhe, the cradle of the Order in the south of France; Eucharist at the women's church in Glendalough, that place of ancient Irish pilgrimage; a poignant moment of grieving as the names and stories of the Sisters who left Ireland for the missions were recalled and remembered during our days together in Tallaght.

Is there, I pondered, a precondition that makes us better able to appreciate the significance of such memories and experiences?

Miriam Rose Ungummerr-Baumann, an Australian Aboriginal elder of the Ngangi-Kurung-Kirr Tribe, speaks of a quality of her people which she names as *dadirri* – an inner, deep listening and quiet, a still awareness. *Dadirri* recognises, she says, the deep spring that is inside us. We call on it and it calls to us. She says it is something like 'what you white people call contemplation.'

Experience of *dadirri* brings wholeness; a big part of it lies in listening, listening to the earth, to nature. Miriam Rose goes on to say that, over thousands of years, her people have listened to their stories. They are told and sung as the seasons go by; and, as the children grow, they become the storytellers and pass on to the young all they must know. The stories and songs, she says, 'sink quietly into our minds and we hold them deep inside.' The ceremonies then celebrated around the stories hold a profound awareness of the sacredness of life. Such an understanding, I know, would be repeated among many cultures which have deep ties with the land. It is important to note, in the way Miriam Rose describes this special contemplative quality, that it is taught, experienced and celebrated in the context of a community.

In his Letter, Peter, recalling his experience, describes the prophetic call to hear God's voice as a call to community. After long years of listening and pondering the mystery of the Father's Word spoken in the Transfigured Son, he urges us to listen so that God's Word becomes 'a lamp for lighting a way through the dark until the dawn comes and the morning star rises in your minds' (v. 19).

And what is the Word, spoken and contemplated in silent listening, calling us to in the present moment? The Transfiguration in the context of Mark's Gospel is embedded in Jesus' invitation to his disciples to take up their cross daily and follow him. It falls between the first and second prophecy of the Passion, when Jesus is headed towards Jerusalem and his crucifixion. Maybe, this story is a good example of the relationship between contemplation and mission: the disciples are taken apart and granted a peak mystical experience, but there is terror and shadow as well as the dazzling white of the transfigured Jesus. They return down the mountain – missioned but filled with disquiet and questions.

It is interesting to me that God speaks out of the shadows. Maybe contemplation has something to do with sitting long enough in the terror of the shadows … Maybe it is something about discerning the shadows that stretch over our land and our people … sitting long enough until God speaks to us … sitting long enough to experience the mystery and the terror.

What are the shadows out of which God is being revealed at present in our lands? We struggle to understand the shadows of our past: the search for national reconciliation, the rise of anti-Islamic paranoia, the scope of sexual abuse across the Churches, the devastating plight of refugees worldwide, the abuse of our natural resources, our willingness to go to war. In the shadows, Jesus is the one who remains to accompany us in our descent down the mountain and in our own journey towards Jerusalem.

It is a journey that calls for deep listening, for a waiting, contemplative spirit. The apostles, while faithful to the warning to be silent about the experience, talked much among themselves about what this 'rising from the dead' could mean. What does it mean for us?

What does rising from the dead mean for our refugee friends interned in camps in the Australian desert and faced with indifference by our own government as well as by much of the voting public? What does rising from the dead mean for both Aboriginal Australians and white Australians? Can we hear Miriam Rose's plea: 'We would like people in Australia to listen to us'? What does rising from the dead mean for our Sisters in the Solomon Islands as they negotiate the ravages of civil war? What does rising from the dead mean for the communities of South Africa as, in wave after wave, they bury mothers and children, and struggle to answer the needs of so many children orphaned by AIDS? What does rising from the dead mean for the Irish people who continue to live and struggle with the deep religious, social and economic divisions imposed upon them by a dark history? What does rising from the dead mean for the millions of poor in Latin America who remain oppressed and alienated by the mighty wealth and power of an elite? What does rising from the dead mean for the people of the United States of America where a culture of obsessiveness about security encloses them in an environment of fear in the midst of freedom?

We know that the disciples did not keep 'the matter to themselves', that they followed Jesus in their own clumsy, human way, and shared in Jesus' passion and death and in the spreading of the good news to different parts of the known world.

As we move into this day and this time to reflect upon the call to contemplation and mission, may we too be strengthened by the presence of Jesus, in our resolve to work for a world where truth and justice meet.

Contributors

Mary C. Daniel, O.P., has been a member St Mary's Dominican Congregation, New Orleans, for forty-three years. The ministry of preaching and accompanying candidates and novices occupy most of her time, together with retreat work and spiritual direction.

Mary Edmund Gibson, O.P., is a member of St Mary's Dominican Congregation, New Orleans. Having been involved in education for many years, as teacher and principal, she is at present Director of Rosaryville Spirit Life Center at 39003 Rosaryville Road, Ponchatoula, Louisiana 70454, U.S.A. She has been in the ministry of hospitality since 1993.

Elizabeth Hellwig, O.P., after years of involvement in deaf education and secondary education, particularly in pastoral care networking, became a professional archivist, almost by accident, in 1991. Since that time she has set up the archives of the Dominican Sisters and the Brothers of St John of God, and assisted several other groups of religious in establishing their archival holdings. Elizabeth has edited and designed a number of publications for the Brothers, and for the Dominican Sisters, including *Up She Gets For Up She Must* – an account of the journey of the first group of Dominican women who came to Australia from Ireland in 1867. Currently Elizabeth is responsible for her congregation's archives and resources for mission, and edits a weekly online newsletter on behalf of the Dominican Family in Australia, New Zealand and the Solomons.

Judith Lawson, O.P., is a member of the Congregation of the Dominican Sisters of Eastern Australia and the Solomon Islands. For some years she has been Principal of Santa Sabina College, a large kindergarten-to-Year-12 school in Sydney, New South Wales.

Rosemary Lewins, O.P., has a long and distinguished history as an educator and administrator. She was principal of Siena and Santa Sabina Secondary Colleges before becoming principal of Signadou College of Education from 1987 to 1990. In 1991, she led the College into the newly established Australian Catholic University, and served as Principal of its Canberra campus until early 1995, at which time she became the University's foundation Dean of Students. Currently she is Prioress of the Dominican Sisters of Eastern Australia and the Solomon Islands.

Margaret MacCurtain, O.P., is a historian, writer and former lecturer in History, and in Women's Studies, University College, Dublin, and former Chair of the National Archive of Ireland. Her publications include (with Donncha Ó Corrain, Eds.), *Women in Irish Society: The Historical Dimension*, Greenwood Publications, USA, 1979, and (with Suellen Troy) *From Dublin to New Orleans: The Journey of Nora and Alice*, Attic Press, Dublin, 1994. She is a much sought-after lecturer at conferences on themes of Irish history and change in contemporary Ireland. She is a sister of the Dominican Congregation, Cabra.

John D'Arcy May, an Australian theologian who has lived in Ireland since 1988, is Associate Professor, Irish School of Ecumenics, Trinity College Dublin, and author of several books on inter-faith dialogue, Pacific Religions, and ethics, including *Living Theology in Melanesia: A Reader*, (Ed.), The Melanesian Institute for Pastoral and Socio-Economic Service, Goroka, Papua New Guinea, 1985; *After Pluralism: Towards an Interreligious Ethic*, LIT, 2000; *Transcendence and Violence: The Encounter of Buddhist, Christian, and Primal Traditions*, Continuum, New York & London, 2003.

Angela Moloney, O.P., is a member of the Dominican Congregation of the Holy Cross, and has lived in Adelaide, South Australia for fifty years. She has a Bachelor of Theology and a Masters of Philosophy in Women's Studies with her thesis work in feminist Christology. She loves to share and to learn with other women from their experiences on life and from their rich resources of feminist and liberation theologies and spiritualities.

Mary O'Driscoll, O.P., is a sister of the Dominican Congregation, Cabra, and Professor of Spiritual and Ecumenical Theology, Pontifical University of St Thomas Aquinas (Angelicum), Rome. She is author of *Passion for the Truth, Compassion for Humanity: Selected Writings of Catherine of Siena,* New City Press, NY, 1993; *Catherine of Siena,* Signe Publications, Strasbourg, 1994; and co-author (with Albert Nolan, O.P.) of *Justice and Truth Shall Meet: Conference Proceedings,* Parable, Sinsinawa, 1984. She is a Roman Catholic representative on the Faith and Order Commission, World Council of Churches, and a highly respected lecturer and retreat director in many parts of the world.

Regina O'Neill, O.P., was born in Tipperary but grew up in Rush, Co. Dublin. She attended Dominican College, Eccles Street, Dublin. She went to Australia in 1950 and joined the Dominicans in Dongara, West Australia. She studied at the University of Western Australia and taught for many years at various secondary schools. She is currently working at Mater Dei College, Joondalup, as Student Counsellor.

Margaret Scharf, O.P., is a member of the Congregation of Dominican Sisters of Western Australia, where she taught for nineteen years in different capacities – in primary school, on 'Motor Mission', and in the Solomon Islands. For the last eight years, she has held several staff positions at the Center for Spiritual Development in Orange, California – as supervisor of the three-year training program for spiritual directors, spiritual director, presenter, liturgist and composer-in-residence.

Geraldine Smyth, O.P., is a sister of the Dominican Congregation, Cabra. She teaches Ecumenical Social Ethics at the Irish

School of Ecumenics, Trinity College Dublin, where she is Senior Lecturer. She is author of *A Way of Transformation*, Peter Lang, Bern, 1995, and joint editor (with Andrew Pierce) of *The Critical Spirit: Theology at the Crossroads of Faith and Culture – Essays in Honour of Gabriel Daly, O.S.A.*, Columba Press, Dublin, 2003, and has contributed articles in a number of books and journals on creation theology and on the theology and politics of peace and reconciliation.

Anne Thurston is a theologian and writer. Author of *Because of Her Testimony: the Word in Female Experience*, Gill and Macmillan, Dublin, 1995, and, *Knowing Her Place: Gender and the Gospels*, Gill and Macmillan, Dublin, 1998, she is also a regular contributor to Irish theological journals on topics which correlate scripture, art, gender and theology. She has lectured widely in Ireland, and recently, in Australia.

Carmel Walsh, O.P., is a New Zealand Dominican sister who has worked in Dominican Colleges and in adult education. Her present role is Dean of Studies at Holy Cross Seminary, and Church History lecturer at Good Shepherd College in Auckland.

Participants

Sr Raymunda Brennan
Cabra Dominicans,[1] South Africa

Sr Catherine Brophy
Dominican Sisters of Western Australia

Sr Mary C. Daniel
Congregation of St Mary, New Orleans

Sr Frances Caine
Dominican Sisters of Eastern Australia and Solomon Islands

Sr Lorraine Challis
New Zealand Dominican Sisters

Sr Raymund Corbett
Cabra Dominicans, Ireland

Sr Teresa Cunningham
Cabra Dominicans, Argentina

Sr Inez Delany
Cabra Dominicans, Ireland

Sr Ann Dolan
Congregation of the Holy Cross/ Cabra, South Australia

Sr Carmel Downes
Cabra Dominicans, Ireland

Sr Julianna Drobik
Dominican Sisters of Eastern Australia and Solomon Islands

Sr Maura Duggan
Cabra Dominicans, Ireland

Sr Barbara Dwyer
New Zealand Dominican Sisters

Sr Aimo Eady
Cabra Dominicans, South Africa

Sr Mary Edmund Gibson
Congregation of St Mary, New Orleans

Sr Gemma Finlay
New Zealand Dominican Sisters

Sr Maude Fitgerald
Cabra Dominicans, South Africa

Sr Odhran Flavin
Cabra Dominicans, Ireland

Sr Cora Gaffney
Cabra Dominicans, Ireland

Sr Frances Gaynor
Congregation of the Holy Cross/ Cabra, South Australia

Sr Caitriona Geraghty
Cabra Dominicans, Ireland

Sr Caitriona Gorman
Cabra Dominicans, Argentina

Sr Elisabeth Healy
Cabra Dominicans, Generalate

Sr Elizabeth Hellwig
Dominican Sisters of Eastern Australia and Solomon Islands

Sr Mary-Clare Holland
Dominican Sisters of Eastern Australia and Solomon Islands

1. Congregation of Dominican Sister, Cabra: with regions in Ireland, Portugal, Southern Africa, Latin America, and Louisiana, USA.

Sr Dominique Horgan
Cabra Dominicans, Ireland
Sr Máire Kealy
Cabra Dominicans, Ireland
Sr Margaret Kelly
Cabra Dominicans, South Africa
Sr Maeve Kelly
Cabra Dominicans, Ireland
Sr Francis Krige
Cabra Dominicans, Generalate
Sr Rita Lane
Cabra Dominicans, Ireland
Sr Marlene Laracy
Dominican Sisters of Western Australia
Sr Angela Lawless
Cabra Dominicans, Ireland
Sr Judith Lawson
Dominican Sisters of Eastern Australia and Solomon Islands
Sr Rosemary Lewins
Dominican Sisters of Eastern Australia and Solomon Islands
Sr Margaret MacCurtain
Cabra Dominicans, Ireland
Sr Veronica McCabe
Cabra Dominicans, Generalate
Sr Maura McAvoy
Dominican Sisters of Eastern Australia and Solomon Islands
Sr Rose McLarnon
Cabra Dominicans, South Africa
Sr Jeanne McLoughlin
Cabra Dominicans, Louisiana

Sr Angela Moloney
Congregation of the Holy Cross/ Cabra, South Australia
Sr Martinez Murphy
Cabra Dominicans, Lisbon
Sr Justina Nutley
Cabra Dominicans, South Africa
Sr Caoimhín Ní Uallacháin
Cabra Dominicans, Ireland
Sr Maureen O'Connell
Congregation of the Holy Cross/ Cabra, South Australia
Sr Maureen O'Connor
Dominican Sisters of Eastern Australia and Solomon Islands
Sr Joseph O'Dea
Cabra Dominicans, Ireland
Sr Mary O'Driscoll
Cabra Dominicans, Generalate
Sr Helen O'Dwyer
Cabra Dominicans, Ireland
Sr Ann O'Neill
New Zealand Dominican Sisters
Sr Deirdre O'Neill
Cabra Dominicans, South Africa
Sr Regina O'Neill
Dominican Sisters of Western Australia
Sr Rose O'Neill
Cabra Dominicans, Ireland
Sr Margaret Purcell
Cabra Dominicans, Ireland
Sr Lorna Ridley
Cabra Dominicans, Ireland

Sr Pauline Riley
*Dominican Sisters of Eastern
Australia and Solomon Islands*

Sr Margaret Scharf
*Dominican Sisters of Western
Australia*

Sr Geraldine Smyth
Cabra Dominicans, Generalate

Sr Elizabeth Smyth
Cabra Dominicans, Brazil

Sr Carmel Walsh
New Zealand Dominican Sisters

Sr Sally Young
Cabra Dominicans, South Africa

Notes

Spanning the Distance
– Dominican Mission Global and Local

1. Richard Sennett, *The Fall of Public Man*, Norton and Co., New York, 1974. Sennett speaks of 'dead public space' and 'neglected public roles', relating an obsession with self to the erosion of social imagination (pp. 3-27). Earlier generations left a legacy of soaring cathedrals, spacious parks and hospitable public squares, which embodied in grass or stone the vision and values of life as civic, communal, and at once, embodied and spiritual. It is said that our legacy will be the glass-domed shopping mall and glass towers of financial enterprise. These are the post-modern places of commerce and worship. Basilicas of urban individualism and consumerism, they mock the human longing for intimacy and for mystery.

2. Geiko Müller-Fahrenholz, 'Will the Earth Remain Habitable?' unpublished lecture delivered at the Irish School of Ecumenics, Dublin, February 2000, with a critical focus on a necessary shift in consciousness towards the world, as from 'domination' to 'indwelling'.

3. See Konrad Raiser, *For a Culture of Life: Transforming a Globalization and Violence*, WCC, Geneva, 2002, p. 3; also, Richard Sennett, *The Uses of Disorder: Personal Identity and City Life*, Faber and Faber, London, 1996; Anthony Giddens, *Modernity and Self-Identity: Self and Society in the Late Modern Age*, Polity Press, Cambridge, 1991, pp. 16-18, 21-27, 200.

4. I acknowledge these insights shared by a friend and colleague, Peter Scherle, who attributes them in turn to Friedrich-Wilhelm Marquardt's theological work on space and utopia, *Eia, Wärn wir da: eine theologische Utopie*, Gütersloe, 1997.

5. See Geraldine Smyth, 'Between the Flood and the Rainbow', in *Doctrine and Life*, Vol. 43, No., 4, 1993, pp. 216-26.

6. Anne Primavesi, *Sacred Gaia: Holistic Theology and Earth System Science*, Foreword by James Lovelock, Routedge, London, 2000, pp. xi-xix and *passim*.

7. Robert J. Schreiter, *Constructing Local Theologies*, S.C.M. Press, London, 1985.

8. Robert J Schreiter, *Reconciliation: Mission and Ministry in a Changing Social Order*, Orbis, New York, 1992.

9. Robert J Schreiter, *The New Catholicity: Theology Between the Global and the Local*, Orbis, New York, 1997. The encounter of cultures thus calls for a 'new Catholicity', which can do justice to the local (social, cultural, political, religious), while holding it in dialectic tension with the global context. It requires us to do theology *between the local and the global*, approaching theology as contextual, plural and inter-contextual, and involving *praxis* as well as theory, following lines of common and shared concern in however diverse ways (pp. 14-27 and *passim*).

10. The seminal work is that of Paul Ricoeur. See, *inter alia, Oneself as Another*, transl. by Kathleen Blamey, University of Chicago Press,

Chicago, 1994, pp. 113-139.

11. Relevant to the purpose in hand, see, for example, the following studies: Sr Mary Augustine McCarthy, O.P., *Mother of the Missions: Mother Mary Gabriel Gill OSD, 1837-1905*, St Dominic's Priory, Dunedin, 1989; Ruth Marchant James, *Fields of Gold: A History of the Dominican Sisters in Western Australia*, Doubleview, Western Australia, 1999; Helen Northey, O.P., *Living the Truth: The Dominican Sisters in South Australia 1868-1958*, Flinders Universtiy of South Australia, Adelaide, 1999; Elizabeth Hellwig, O.P. (ed.), *Up She Gets, For Up She Must! An Account of a Journey from Kingstown, Ireland to Maitland, Australia in 1867, during the Age of Sail*, Dominican Sisters of Eastern Australia and the Solomon Islands, Strathfield, NSW, 2001; *Our Irish Sisters: 1867-1888: Who Helped Found the Congregation of Dominican Sisters of Eastern Australia and the Solomon Islands*, Dominican Archives, Strathfield, New South Wales, 2003; Mary Nona McGreal, O.P. (ed.), *Dominicans at Home in a Young Nation 1786-1865, Vol. 1*, Editions du Signe, Strasbourg, 2001; *Weavings: Celebrating Dominican Women*, Dublin, 1998 (n.d.); Kathleen Boner, O.P., *Dominican Women: A Time to Speak*, Cluster Publications, Pietermaritzburg, 2000; Sr Rose O'Neill, O.P., *A Rich Inheritance: Galway Dominican Nuns 1644-1994*, Galway, 1994 (n.d.); Mary O'Byrne, O.P., *Strands from a Tapestry: A Story of Dominican Sisters in Latin America*, Dominican Publications, Dublin, 2001; Margaret Mac Curtain and Donncha O'Corrain, Eds., *Women in Irish Society: the Historical Dimension*, Greenwood Publications, U.S.A. 1979; Margaret Mac Curtain, O.P., and Mary Ellen O'Dowd, *Women in Early Modern Ireland*, Edinburgh University Press, Edinburgh, 1991; Suellen Troy and Margaret MacCurtain O.P., *From Dublin to New Orleans: the Journey of Nora and Alice*, Attic Press, Dublin, 1994. Desmond Forristal, *The Siena Story, 1722-1997*, Monastery of St Catherine, Drogheda, Ireland, 1997.

12. Julia Kristeva, 'Women's Time', in *A Kristeva Reader*, Ed., Toril Moi, Columbia, N.Y., 1986, pp. 187-213. Here, Kristeva is reclaiming the experience and discourse of motherhood, not as a counter to male experience with its predilection for linear historic time, but insisting on the need for a reconciliation of these approaches (the central logic of her argument forbids this or any other such claim to one identity as 'sum total'), with a view to inclusiveness and transformation for women, men and children. The symbol of having been born, if not of actually giving birth touches into something universal, but here Kristeva posits it as an invitation to love an other in attentiveness and self-forgetfulness (p. 206).

13. See, Timothy Radcliffe O.P., 'Religious Life in the World That Is Coming to Be', Address to National Assembly of CCSM, Louisville, U.S., 2003, http://www.op.org/domcentral/library/coming2b.htm, pp. 1-10. Here, the former Master of the Dominican Order presents the vowed religious life in terms of a communion, requiring neither money nor power, whose power is sacramental and symbolic rather than substantial or dominant, and witnessing to a form of belonging that is radically different from what is on offer at the global commun-

ion tables of MacDonald's or Burger King: 'Every Eucharist is the re-enactment of hope lost and renewed. Every Eucharist makes visible a crisis of power lost and regained. It shows us the extinction and renewal of promise. The end of the road becomes the beginning of the way to the Kingdom' (p. 4). It is interesting that these observations addressed to an all-male body of religious finds echoes and resonance in Kristeva's feminist perspectives.

14. See also, John D'Arcy May, *Transcendence and Violence: The Encounter of Buddhist, Christian and Primal Traditions*, Continuum, New York and London, 2003, pp. 25-41, where the author gives a more extensive treatment of the colonizing of Australia as a confronting of 'the Primal Other', with the implied 'critique of European completeness', and (quoting Robert Hughes), ironically linked with Europeans' discovery of their own 'geographical unconscious'.

15. Walter Brueggemann, *Hope Within History*, John Knox Press, Atlanta, 1987, pp. 49-71. Here, Brueggemann puts forward a radical counter-history, marshalling the proclamations of the prophetic tradition, that 'formal power-holders' are not automatically 'the history-makers.' On the contrary, history-making is achieved through 'the voice of marginality' (p. 55), through the witness of those who have the capacity and courage to disclose the human processes of domination, hurt and anger, but who also know that it is at the edges of society that 'alternatives are thinkable... in terms of imagination not yet co-opted' (p. 69).

16. Unidentified Guest in, *The Cocktail Party*, Act One, Scene 3, in *T.S. Eliot: The Complete Poems and Plays*, Faber and Faber, London, 1969, p. 385.

17. Paul Ricoeur, *Interpretation Theory: Discourse and the Surplus of Meaning*, Texas Christian University Press, Forth Worth, 1976, pp. 87 ff.

18. Walter Benjamin, 'Thesis VII', *Illuminations*, Fontana, HarperCollins, London, 1973, pp 247-248. Benjamin, fleeing with other Jewish refugees from Nazi-occupied France, was refused entry at the border-crossing into Spain. Told that their passports were not in order, they were kept overnight, to be sent back the following day – to certain death. But Benjamin took his own life while still in custody - a factor, undoubtedly, in influencing the authorities to let the others through. See, Michael P. Steinberg, Ed., *Walter Benjamin and the Demands of History*, Cornell University Press, N.Y., 1996, pp. 210-3. In brushing against the cultural grain, the underlying purpose is to release the critical and subversive elements in the received tradition, not simply to arrive at a counter-cultural, but rather a 'redemptive reading' that gives due attention to history *and* critique (ibid., pp. 4-5).

19. Walter Benjamin, *Illuminations*, p. 248.

20. It is also true that our location as *homo sapiens* usually overlooks the other-than-human creation (which has preceded us by millions of years), wiping out the existence and significance of the myriad galaxies beyond our ken in the whole created universe. There is much to be learned, in this regard, from Indigenous Traditions. Cf., for example, George Tinker (a Native American Theologian), 'Creation as Beloved by God', in *Echoes*, 1996, No 10, WCC Publications, Geneva, pp. 19-22;

also, Dan O'Donovan, *Dadirri*, Nelen Yubu Missiological Unit, Kensington, Australia, 2001, on the Aboriginal idea of contemplation, presented first by Miriam Rose, as an 'inner, deep listening' which acknowledges the whole universe as sacramental it is akin to contemplation and 'the greatest gift we can give to our fellow Australians' (p. 21, and *passim*); see also the 'Chiang Mai Affirmation of Indigenous Peoples', in *Current Dialogue*, 2000, pp 42-44.

21. Cf. Richard Falk, *Predatory Globalization: A Critique*, Polity Press, Cambridge, 1999, pp. 146149.

22. Richard Falk, ibid., pp. 148-149. These form an interesting overlap with Robert Schreiter's 'global theological flows', outlined below, offering some middle axioms which can help to structure collaborative thinking and practice, with other disciplines, secular bodies and NGOs; see also, 'Globalization as Challenge and Opportunity in Global Mission: an Outlook from London' in, *International Review of Mission*, Vol. LXXXVIII, No., 351, October 1999, pp. 381-389, especially with reference to the effects on space, worked out in relation to 'utopia, cosmopolis and Kingdom', p. 385, and the linking of '*glocalization* [sic] and sustainability', according to the New Testament image of the 'householding of faith', pp. 386-388.

23. Will Hutton, *The World We Are In*, Little Brown, London, 2002; also, Will Hutton and Anthony Giddens, Eds., *On the Edge: Living With Global Capitalism*, Vintage Press, London, 2001.

24. Zygmunt Bauman, *Globalization: the Human Consequences*, Polity Press, Cambridge, 1998, pp. 2-4, and especially Chapter 2, 'Space Wars: a Career Report', pp. 27-54; also, Richard Sennett, *The Uses of Disorder, in which* the author exposes the self-serving nostalgia of 'slum romantics' and the new purified intensity of family-based social life in which the wealthy withdraw to their protected suburbanised islands with their 'brutal functional simplicity' that marginalizes the poor; swallows up public spaces; and seals off possibilities for encounter with those leading diverse lives, and opportunities to explore and wander. Such chosen impotence is then moralized as 'protecting' family and children (pp. 82-4).

25. The massive anti-globalization rallies, surrounding G8 / World Trade meetings in Seattle (1999) or Genoa (2001), and, as this goes to press, the collapse of negotiations at the World Trade Summit at Cancun, Mexico) demonstrates the increasing scale of resistance to the implacable laws of the global economy. For an accessible and comprehensive analysis, which argues for an ethical approach to global trade, interrelating, economic, geo-political and theological perspectives (e.g., trade and peace, trade and jobs, trade and religions, trade and cultures, trade and human rights) see, Christoph Stückelberger, *Global Trade Ethics: an Illustrated Overview*, with a Preface by Rubens Ricupero, UNCTAD, WCC, Geneva, 2002.

26. Samuel Huntington, *The Clash of Civilisations*, Simon and Schuster, N.Y., 1996. This was dismissed by John Pilger, as 'a *Reader's Digest* View of the World'. It may well be, but Huntington's reductionist interpretation of world politics has been mightily influential in shap-

ing contemporary militant US foreign policy. It can be argued that it has been a major factor in post-Cold War international relations analysis, premised not on the real world 'out there', but on the need to find or even invent a new enemy, as justification for U.S hegemony in world affairs. See, Michael Cox, 'International History since 1989', in John Baylis and Steve Smith, Eds., *The Globalization of World Politics: An Introduction to International Relations*, Oxford University Press, 2001, pp. 111-137, pp. 115-116.

27. See David A. Kerr, 'Christian Mission and Islamic Studies: Beyond Antithesis', in *International Bulletin of Missionary Research*, Vol. 26, No., 1, January 2002, pp. 81-5. There is, incidentally, alongside this historically-based article, a full page listing of 'Centres for the Study of Islam and Christian-Muslim Relations' (p. 12).

28. For all the attention being called to the dangers entailed in the radicalisation of the Muslim rhetoric of '*jihad*' ('holy struggle'), there is a comparable phenomenon in contemporary political rhetoric in the U.S., often couched in unexamined Christian assumptions of a particularist kind, such as, pre-destined election and righteousness, blended uncritically with transcending images of military dogma (might as right), rather than to the other Western political diction of democratic freedom and self-determination. Cf. Ibrahim Warde, 'Which God is on Whose Side?' *Monde Diplomatique,* September 2002; also, Arthur Schlesinger, 'The Theory of America: Experiment or Destiny' in *The Cycles of American History*, Houghton Mifflin, 1987.

29. John de Gruchy and Charles Villa-Vicencio, eds, *Apartheid is a Heresy*, David Philip Publisher (Pty), Cape Town and Eerdmans Publishers, Grand Rapids, 1983, which includes a number of statements on the part of churches in and beyond South Africa, who found it necessary to repudiate – in explicit theological terms - the prevailing theological justifications for *apartheid.*

30. His ecclesiology of 'all in each place' was a formulation characterized by the Fifth General Assembly of the World Council of Churches in Nairobi, 1975. This emphasis on the local church accords with Vatican II, but has recently come into some contention in the Roman Catholic church, as will be seen below.

31. Robert J. Schreiter, *The New Catholicity*, pp. 14-21. 'The discourse of liberation, feminism, ecology and human rights as global theological flows address the contradictions and failures of global systems', but they can lay claim to being the new 'universal' theologies, not out of the grandiose claims linked to Enlightenment theologies, but ' … in their ubiquity, and in their addressing of universal , systemic problems affecting nearly everyone in the world'. (p. 20). One could with foundation add ecumenism and communications to Shreiter's four.

32. *The New Catholicity*, p. 15. The 'flow' is a term used in the disciplines of anthropology, sociology and communications theory.

33. Rachel Carson, *The Edge of the Sea*, New American Library, New York, 1995, p. 215.

34. See Walter Kasper, 'On the Church: a Friendly Reply to Cardinal Ratzinger', in *The Furrow*, Vol., 52, No. 6, June 2001, pp. 323-332. Here

the President of the Pontifical Council for Christian Unity, challenges Cardinal Ratzinger's claims on the ontological primacy of the church universal, arguing the historic weakness of the Cardinal's claim and also insisting *contra* Ratzinger, that the theological pre-eminence of the church applies not only to the universal church, but also to local churches (p. 330). For purposes of our argument, it is useful to underline Kasper's setting out of Vatican II ecclesiology, on which points he and Ratzinger, in fact, agree: 1. 'Jesus Christ wanted only one single church.. The one church of Christ 'subsists' in the Roman Catholic Church ...2 The one church of Jesus Christ exists 'in and from' the local churches... [as] each local church exists 'in and from' the one church of Jesus Christ' in communion with all other local churches... [and] 3. just as] the local churches are not mere extensions or provinces of the universal church, so the universal church is not the mere sum of the local churches. *The local churches and the universal church are intimately united. They share the same existence; they live within each other'*, (p. 329, italics mine).

35. Walter Brueggeman, op. cit., p. 20.

36. It is significant that the now existence of D.S.I. as a global structure was forged at the time of the first Gulf War in 1991, out of a similar desire of Dominican women in the West to be in solidarity with their 'Dominican Family' in Iran and Iraq whose plight was till then barely known to them. Through communication, visits, prayer partnerships and other processes of solidarity, D.S.I. emerged, as a global body with more than thirty thousand Dominican Women, and over one hundred and sixty distinct congregations, as a federation, which has given new impetus to the vision and responsibility of a shared history, of similar strands in ministry – prayer and preaching, justice and peace, option for the poor, care of the earth, ecumenical and inter-cultural dialogue, feminist theology, human rights - all reflecting an facet of St Dominc's founding charism. Cf., *Dominican Sisters International: Interim Report*, October 2002, Rome, 2002, dsi@curia.op.org; see also, http://www.op/dsi.

37. See, Anthony J. Gittins, *Reading the Clouds: Mission Spirituality for New Times*, St Pauls, Strathfield, New South Wales, 1999, pp. ix-xiii, and *passim*.

38. *Vatican II: Constitution, Decrees Declarations*, Gen. Ed., Austin Flannery, Dominican Publications, Dublin, 1996, pp. 443-497.

39. There was also an emphasis on the permanent priority of missions in the Roman Catholic Church's commitment to evangelization (a fea-ture also in John Paul II's *Redemptoris Missio* (Mission of the Redeemer, 1991).

40. David J. Bosch, *Transforming Mission: Paradigm Shifts in Theology of Mission*, Orbis, N.Y, 1991, must earn the claim to being the magisterial overview in this field. The author examines five paradigms of mission in the course of the Christian tradition and understanding of mission, and outlines the features of an emerging 'ecumenical missionary paradigm' in terms of a dialectic relationship between salvation's transcendent and immanent dimensions (pp. 368-510). See also, Donal

Dorr, *Mission in Today's World* Columba Press, Dublin, 2001; also, Robert J. Schreiter, Ed., *Mission in the Third Millennium*, Orbis, N.Y., 2001, esp. pp. 121-161 and *passim*. The volume represents perspectives from different cultures and traditions constituted around a SEDOS conference on the theme, Rome, 2000; also, *Mission: an Ecumenical Introduction – Texts and Contexts of Global Christianity*, Eds., F.J. Verstraelen (General Editor), A. Camps, L.A. Hoedemaker, and M.R. Spindler, Eerdmans, Grand Rapids, 1995; Maria Rieckleman, 'My Pilgrimage in Mission', in *International Bulletin of Missionary Research*, Vol., 25, No. 4, 2001, pp. 169-173..

41. For a recent Dominican reflection on mission as, 'presence', 'epiphany' and 'proclamation', see, Timothy Radcliffe OP, 'Mission to a Runaway World: Future Citizens of the Kingdom', Address to SEDOS Missionary Conference, 2000, also found in, Timothy Radcliffe OP, *I Call You Friends*, Continuum, N.Y., pp. 128-142.

42. See Anne Primavesi, *Sacred Gaia*, especially Chapter 8, 'Justice North and South', pp. 81-92.

43. It is significant that many other world Church bodies are taking up this issue (or nexus of issues) as a priority. For example, the Union of Major Superiors International (U.I.S.G.) puts it at the core of its current strategic vision, with a particular emphasis on women and children. The reality of trafficking in women and children was also the theme of the Council of European Churches (C.E.C) meeting in Prague, 2003, focussing attention on women and children coming (or being brought) from Eastern Europe, North Africa and Asia especially. See also the quarterly newsletter series on *Uprooted People*, International Relations Team, WCC, Geneva, 9 Oct. 1999 and subsequently; available also via WCC website: http://wcc-coe.org

44. The 'Ethical Globalization Initiative: New Venture to Support Human Rights' has recently been founded in New York with Mary Robinson as its first Director. Cf. also her 'Linking Ethical and Globalisation', in *Between Poetry and Politics: Essays in Honour of Enda McDonagh*, edited by Linda Hogan and Barbara FitzGerald, Columba Press, Dublin, 2003, pp. 182-90.

45. Cited in Olivia O'Leary and Helen Burke, *Mary Robinson: the Authorised Biography*, Hodder and Stoughton, London, 1998, p. 186.

46. Moya Cannon, 'Migrations' in *The Parchment Boat*, Gallery Press, Oldcastle, Ireland, 1997, p. 42.

Tending the Wells of Memory
– Sharing Sources of Hope

1. Mary Robinson, Inaugural Address. See printed text in Fergus Finlay, *Mary Robinson, a President with a Purpose*, O'Brien Press, Dublin, 1990, pp. 155-66.

2. Olivia O'Leary and Helen Burke, *Mary Robinson: the Authorised Biography*, Hodder & Stoughton, London, 1998, pp.138-9; see Chapter 17, 'The Forgotten People', pp. 189-205.

3. Ray Mac Mánais, *Máire Mhic Ghiolla Íosa: Beathaisnéis*, Cló Iar- Chon-

nachta, Indreabhán, Connamara, 2003, pp. 38-54; Remarks made by President of Ireland , Mary McAleese , at the Australian Memorial to the Famine, Hyde Park Barracks, Sydney, 13 March 2003. Press-office, Áras an Uachtaráin.

4. Remarks by President McAleese at the Australian Irish Society's St Patrick's Day Ball, Sydney ,15 March 2003. Press-office, Áras an Uachtaráin.

5. Andrew Higgins Wyndham, Introduction, *Re-Imagining Ireland : Transformations of Identity in a Global Context*, programme notes for a Conference held in Virginia Foundation for the Humanities, Charlottesville, 7-10 May 2003.

6. Suellen Hoy, 'The Journey Out: The Recruitment and Emigration of Irish Religious Women to the United States, 1812-1914' in *Journal of Women's History*, 1995, vol 6, no 4.

7. In conversation with Maureen McMahon, O.P., artist, on the choice of the logo.

8. Honor Mc Cabe is currently researching for publication a full history of the convent of Bom Sucesso and its community, 1639 —.

9. I am indebted to Maura Duggan, O.P., who has researched nineteenth-century Dominican communities in Ireland and overseas.

10. Elizabeth Hellwig, O.P., *Up She Gets, For Up She Must! An Account of a Journey from Kingstown, Ireland to Maitland, Australia in 1867 during the Age of Sail*, Dominican Publications, Maitland, 2001.

11. Loc.cit., p. 82

12. Walter Nugent, *Crossings: The Great Transatlantic Migrations,1870-1914*, Indiana University Press, Bloomington,1992.

13. Suellen Hoy and Margaret MacCurtain, *From Dublin to New Orleans: The Journey of Nora and Alice*, Attic Press, Dublin 1994, p. 17

14. Monica Devers, O.P., Helen Mc Ging, O.P., Patrice de Burgh, O.P. and Clare Donnelly, O.P., designed and carried out the art-work for the panel for the Dominican Congregation, Cabra (cover design).

15. Maria Mackey, O.P., 'The Black Madonna' in *The Presence and Other Poems*, Dominican Region House, St John Street, Cape Town, 2003, p. 32.

16. Marian O'Sullivan, O.P., Preface, in Kathleen Boner, *Dominican Women: a Time to Speak*, Cluster Publications, Pietermaritzburg, 2000, p. ix.

17. Suellen Hoy, art. cit., pp. 66-83.

18. In conversation with Maura Duggan, O.P.

19. Áine Hardiman, Text in *Dominican Women: A Time to Speak*, pp. 333-34.

20. Edward Schillebeeckx, 'The Golden Thread Dominican Spirituality, A Tribute to the Memory of Dr Finbar Ryan, O.P.', delivered 27 February 1983, Dominican Convent, Cabra, Dublin.

21. Emily Dickinson, *The Complete Poems of Emily Dickinson*, Faber and Faber Ltd, London, 1977, p. 253.

In Praise of Valiant Women:
Women and the Word

1. *Wisdom Ways: Introducing Feminist Biblical Interpretation* (Maryknoll:

Orbis Books, 2001) p. 57.

2. Carol Ann Duffy, 'Anon' in *Feminine Gospels* (London: Picador, 2002)

3. These methods are detailed in her many works from *Bread Not Stone: The Challenge of Biblical Interpretation* (Edinburgh: T&T Clarke, 1984) to the recently published *Wisdom Ways* (2001).

4. Phyllis Trible, 'Out of the Shadows', *Bible Review*, Vol.1:1 (February 1989) pp. 14-25, 34; and also 'Subversive Justice: Tracing the Miriamic Traditions in Justice and the Holy' in *Essays in Honour of Walter Harrelson*, ed. Douglas A. Knight and Peter J. Paris (Atlanta: Scholars Press, 1989).

5. Charlotte Perkins Gilman, cited in Maria Harris, *Women and Teaching:* 1998 Madeleva Lecture in Spirituality (New York: Paulist Press, 1998)

6. Barbara Kingsolver, *Small Wonder: Essays.* (London: Faber&Faber, 2002).

7. 'Subversive Justice', pp. 102-3; and for example Richard Clifford, S.J., in his commentary on Exodus in *The New Jerome Biblical Commentary* (London: Geoffery Chapman, 1990) p. 50.

8. 'Subversive Justice', p. 107.

9. Phyllis Trible, 'Meeting Mary through Luke' http://www.pulpit.org/articles/meeting_mary.asp

10. Gerald O'Collins, 'Peter's Good News at Easter', *The Tablet* 11/18 April 1998.

11. Sandra M. Schneiders, *Written That You May Believe: Encountering Jesus in the Fourth Gospel* (New York: Herder and Herder, Crossroad, 1999).

12. Rosemary Radford Ruether, 'No Church Conspiracy against Mary Magdalene', *The National Catholic Reporter*, February 9, 2001.

13. For this and other information about the history of devotion to Mary Magdalene my primary source has been Susan Haskins, *Mary Magdalene, Myth and Metaphor* (New York: Riverhead Books, 1993) p. 131.

14. Cited in Haskins., p. 131

15. Ruether op. cit., and Haskins op. cit.

16. Cited in Haskins, p. 152

17. Documented in *The Field Day Anthology of Irish Writing Volume V: Irish Women's Writing and Traditions*, edited Angela Bourke, Siobhán Kilfeather, Maria Luddy, Margaret MacCurtain, Geraldine Meaney, Máirín Ní Dhonnachadha, Mary O'Dowd, and Clair Willis, 2002, Cork, Cork University Press 2002) pp. 736-51.

18. See the recent film on the subject, *The Magdalene Sisters*, directed by Peter Mullen, 2003; and the repeated documentary on the Amgdale laundries, RTÉ Radio One, produced by Julian Vignoles, May 28 2003

19. Thomas N. Burke (1830-82) from 'Lectures on Faith and Fatherland' (1874) in *The Field Day Anthology V*. 744.

20. Barbara E. Reid, *Choosing the Better Part? Women in the Gospel of Luke* (Collegeville Minnesota, A Michael Glazier Book. Liturgical Press, 1996) pp. 124-134; 198-204. Mary Catherine Hilkert, *Naming Grace: Preaching and the Sacramental Imagination* (New York: Continuum, 1997) pp.144-65.

21. Reid, op. cit., p. 125.

22. Sandra M. Schneiders, *The Revelatory Text: Interpreting the New Testament as Sacred Scripture* (San Francisco: HarperCollins 1991), p. 188; a comment made with reference to the Samaritan Woman (John 4) but equally applicable here.
23. Reid, op. cit., p. 133.
24. A point acknowledged in the introduction to her feastday in *The Weekday Missal* (London: HarperCollins, 1982) p. 1587. The lectionary readings were changed to reflect the understanding in the Roman Missal that the woman in Luke 7 and Mary Magdalene were no longer considered to be the same person.
25. For example, Mathis Grunewald, 'Crucifixion', from the Isenheim Altarpiece, 1510-16; Giotto, 'Crucifixion', Padua, 1305; or Rubens, 'The Descent from the Cross with the Red Robed Magdalene', 1611, Courtald Institute Galleries, London.
26. Schneiders, *Written that You May Believe*. p. 192.
27. Ibid., p. 195.
28. Hilkert. *Naming Grace*, p. 145.
29. Schneiders op. cit., p. 196.
30. Ibid., p. 199.
31. John Drury, *Painting the Word: Christian Pictures and their Meanings* (New Haven and London: Yale University Press, 1999) p. 118.
32. Yet, one must wonder at the selection from the lectionary for the Gospel on Easter Sunday when the reading from John terminates at verse 9 and does not include the commission to Mary Magdalene.
33. Mary Collins in *Women at Prayer: 1987 Madeleva Lecture in Women's Spirituality* (Mahwah: Paulist Press, 1987) refers to this place where Jewish women gather to reimagine what the Bible does not record.
34. Schneiders op. cit., p. 200.
35. Hilkert, *Naming Grace*, p.183.
36. Phyllis Trible, Santa Clara Lecture, Santa Clara University, April 27, 1997 – http://www.scu.edu/bannancenter/SantaClaraLectures/TribleLecture.htm.
37. Ibid. 2.
38. Ibid. 3.
39. Ibid. 7.
40. Ibid. 9.

The Space In Between
– Mission as Reconciliation

1. Now published as: Joseph Liechty and Cecelia Clegg, *Moving Beyond Sectarianism: Religion, Conflict, and Reconciliation in Northern Ireland* (Dublin: Columba Press, 2001).
2. An example is the not uncontroversial work of the Lutheran missionary Christian Keysser in New Guinea, who aimed at the integral evangelisation of entire ethnic groups rather than concentrating on individual conversions; see Theodor Ahrens, 'Die Aktualität Christian Keyssers. Eine Fallstudie protestantischer Mission', *id.*, *Der neuer Mensch im kolonialen Zwielicht. Studien zum religiösen Wandel in Ozeanien*

(Münster-Hamburg: Lit Verlag, 1993), pp. 29-44; and, on the Church that eventually emerged from the Lutheran mission to Melanesia, Herwig Wagner and Hermann Reiner, eds., *The Lutheran Church in Papua New Guinea: The First Hundred Years 1886-1986* (Adelaide: Lutheran Publishing House, 1986).

3. For a dramatic study of an indigenous Church thrust into 'real' as opposed to 'formal' independence, see Theodor Ahrens, 'Melanesian Christianity Between and Betwixt the Local and the Global', *id.*, *Grace and Reciprocity: Missiological Studies* (Goroka, Papua New Guinea: The Melanesian Institute, Point Series No. 26, 2002), pp. 116-130.

4. See Walter Kardinal Kasper, 'Ökumene zwischen Ost und West. Stand und Perspektiven des Dialogs mit den orthodoxen Kirchen', *Stimmen der Zeit* 2003/3, pp. 150-164, 155-8.

5. See Robert Schreiter, *The New Catholicity: Theology Between the Global and the Local* (Maryknoll: Orbis Books, 1997). The term 'real virtuality' was coined by Manuel Castells; see J.D. May, 'God in Public: The Religions in Pluralist Societies', *Bijdragen* [forthcoming]; *id.*, 'Contested Space: Alternative Models of the Public Sphere in the Asia-Pacific', Neil Brown and Robert Gascoigne, eds., *Faith in the Public Forum* (Adelaide: Australian Theological Forum, 1999), pp. 78-108.

6. See Catherine Cornille, ed., *Many Mansions? Multiple Religious Belonging and Christian Identity* (Maryknoll: Orbis Books, 2002).

7. The Irish School of Ecumenics, Trinity College Dublin, has inaugurated an M.Phil. programme in Reconciliation Studies, taught in Belfast; see J.D. May, 'A Rationale for Reconciliation', *Uniting Church Studies* 7/1 (2001), pp. 1-13.

8. See J.D. May, 'Realised Catholicity: The Incarnational Dimension of Multiculturalism', *The Australasian Catholic Record* 76 (1999),pp. 419-29.

9. Quoted by Walter Wink, *Engaging the Powers: Discernment and Resistance in a World of Domination* (Minneapolis: Fortress Press, 1992), p. 216.

10. The theme runs through the missiological reflections of Theodor Ahrens, *Mission nachdenken. Studien* (Frankfurt: Verlag Otto Lembeck, 2002), esp. 26-27, 34, 105-106 and the concluding essay, 'Das Kreuz mit der Gewalt. Religiöse Dimensionen der Gewaltproblematik', pp. 199-232.

11. Reading the Book of Isaiah in the weeks prior to and during the Second Gulf War in early 2003 I was powerfully reminded of the long history of religiously sanctioned violence in the Middle East. Regina Schwartz, prompted by her student's remark: 'What about the Canaanites?', was similarly moved to write *The Curse of Cain: The Violent Legacy of Monotheism* (Chicago and London: University of Chicago Press, 1997).

12. See the controversy between Theodor Ahrens, 'On Grace and Reciprocity: A Fresh Approach to Contextualisation with Reference to Christianity in Melanesia', *id.*, *Grace and Reciprocity*, pp. 360-80, and Ennio Mantovani, *International Review of Mission* 90 (2001), pp. 462-4, replying to the original publication of Ahrens's article in that journal,

IRM 89 (2000), pp. 515-28, and my discussion of the problem in J.D. May, *Transcendence and Violence: The Encounter of Buddhist, Christian and Primal Traditions* (New York and London: Continuum, 2003), pp. 59-61.

13. This is the well known thesis of René Girard, *Violence and the Sacred* (Baltimore and London: Johns Hopkins University Press, 1977), which I for one find unconvincing as an interpretation of the New Testament, and exaggerated as an explanation of the origin of all religion, despite Girard's immense learning and fascinating textual analyses. See the discerning remarks of Wink, *Engaging the Powers*, pp. 152-5.

14. See Wink, *Engaging the Powers*, chapter 11, and my discussion in J.D. May, *After Pluralism: Towards and Interreligious Ethic* (Münster-Hamburg: Lit Verlag, 2000), pp. 23-9.

15. This is the title of an incisive study of the theology of forgiveness by Geiko Müller-Fahrenholz, *Vergebung macht frei. Vorschläge für eine Theologie der Versöhnung* (Frankfurt: Verlag Otto Lembeck, 1996); the English version, *The Art of Forgiveness: Theological Reflections on Healing and Reconciliation* (Geneva: World Council of Churches, 1997), is not so much a translation as a re-writing of the original.

16. These misconceptions have been helpfully clarified by Robert Schreiter, *Reconciliation: Mission and Ministry in a Changing Social Order* (Maryknoll: Orbis Books, 1992), pp. 18-27.

17. No one, to my mind, has brought this out more vividly and convincingly than Marc Gopin, *Between Eden and Armageddon: The Future of World Religions, Violence, and Peacemaking* (Oxford: Oxford University Press, 2000). Gopin speaks of the 'prosocial' potential of religions (p. 59), noting, however, that what the parties to religiously-inspired conflicts fear most is 'cultural annihilation by assimilation' (p. 175).

18. This is a key thesis of Müller-Fahrenholz, *The Art of Forgiveness*, whose argument I summarise in what follows.

19. Ahrens, *Mission nachdenken* (pp. 224-5): 'Die Liebe erlöst, indem sie das Böse nicht vergilt. ... Wenn Gott nicht wirklich vergeben könnte, dann wäre er in der Tat ohnmächtig gegenüber dem Gesetz der Retribution'.

20. See R. Scott Appleby, *The Ambivalence of the Sacred: Religion, Violence, and Reconciliation* (Lanham, Boulder, New York, Oxford: Rowman & Littlefield, 2000), for an impressive survey of the religions' peacemaking potential.

21. See Gopin, *Between Eden and Armageddon*, pp. 202-3.

Renewing the Dominican Vision
– 'A Passion of Possibility'

1. Søren Kierkegaard, 'The Moment,' in *Kierkegaard's Writings*, vol.23, ed. Hong,1998, Princeton, Princeton University Press.

2. Cf. IDI no.410, March 2003.

3. 'Homage to a Saint' in *The Way of the Preacher*, 1979, London, Darton Longman and Todd, pp. xiv-xv.

4. M. H.Vicaire, *St Dominican and His Times*, Darton Longman and Todd,

London, 1964, pp. 118-32.
5. See Veseley, *Il Secondo Ordine*, doctoral thesis, Angelicum University, Rome.
6. Aniceto Fernandez, *Letter to the Order on the Occasion of the Declaration of Catherine of Siena as a Doctor of the Church*, 1970.
7. John Paul II, Apostolic Letter, Eng. Ed.in *L'Osservatore Romano*, Rome English edition, 40 (1611).
8. Raymond of Capua, *The Life of Catherine of Siena*, 1980, Dublin, Dominican Publications, Part II, Chapter 1, 122.
9. See, S. Tugwell, *Early Dominicans*, Paulist Press.
10. K.Boner, *Dominican Women, a Time to Speak*, Cluster Publications, Pietermaritzburg, 2000, p. 91.
11. See Jordan of Saxony, *On the Beginnings of the Order of Preachers*, 1982, Dublin, Dominican Publications, n. 7.
12. See 'De Vita Intellectuali', Chapter 3 of the *Acta of the General Chapter of the Order of Preachers*, 2001.

RESPONSE *Unimaginable Journeyings*
Dominican Sisters of Eastern Australia and the Solomon Islands

1. What is now the Congregation of Dominican Sisters of Eastern Australia and the Solomon Islands was founded from St Mary's Dominican Convent, Kingstown/Dun Laoghaire, in Maitland New South Wales, 10th September 1867.
2. Cf. also Genevieve Mooney, O.P., 'Mrs Bellew's Family in Channel Row', paper read to the Old Dublin Society, 22 February, 1967.
3. See, Elizabeth Hellwig, O.P., *Up She Gets, For Up She Must! An Account of a Journey from Kingstown, Ireland to Maitland, Australia in 1867 during the Age of Sail*, Dominican Sisters of Eastern Australia and the Solomon Islands, 2001.
4. Joan Chittister, O.S.B., *A Passion for Life: Fragments of the Face of God;* illustrations by Robert Lentz, Orbis Books 1996, p. 130.

RESPONSE *A Tapestry Explored*
Dominican Sisters of South Australia

1. See panel facing p. 65.
2. See Helen Northey, *Living the Truth, the Dominican Sisters in South Australia 1868-1958*, Flinders University of South Australia and Holy Cross Congregation of Dominican Sisters, South Australia, Press, 1999.
2. Anne Henderson, *Mary MacKillop's Sisters: A Life Unveiled*, Harper-Collins Publishers, Australia, 1997, p. viii. Mary MacKillop founded the Congregation of St Joseph in 1867.
3. Cf. the *Sophia* website: www.sophia.org.au
4. One night a group of Anglican women were accidentally locked in the Sophia grounds which are adjacent to the cemetery where all the deceased Sisters are buried. These women put their experience to creative use by composing a song called 'The Dead Sisters' – a joyful expression of the Communion of Saints.

RESPONSE
'Do for God What the Miners Do for Gold'
Dominican Sisters of Aotearoa-New Zealand, 1871-2003

1. The invitation to work in the newly created bishopric of Dunedin, on the South Island of New Zealand, had come from Bishop Patrick Moran, a native of Dublin and a friend of the Sisters in Sion Hill, Dublin. Prior to his appointment to Dunedin, Dr Moran had been Titular Bishop of Dardania, with responsibility for the administration of the Eastern Vicariate of the Cape of Good Hope, South Africa, which centred on Grahamstown.
2. Mark Twain, *Mark Twain in Australia and New Zealand*, Penguin, Victoria, 1973, p. 287.
3. M.M. Francis to Prioress, Sion Hill, 17 March 1871. Sion Hill Archives (SHA).
4. Ibid.
5. Ibid.
6. M.M. Francis to Prioress, Sion Hill, 17 March 1871. SHA
7. S.M. de Ricci to Dr. Kirby, 8 July 1872, Irish College, Rome, Archives.
8. M.M. Gabriel to M.M. Clare, Sion Hill, 21 May 1880, SHA
9. S.M. Louis to Prioress, 22 February 1905, SHA
10. The Rule of St Augustine was chosen by St Dominic in 1216 for his newly founded Order.
11. M.M. Reginald to Sisters, 22 February 1935, (New Zealand Dominican Sisters Archives) NZDSA.

RESPONSE *'Old Friends Are Best'*
Dominican Sisters of Western Australia

1. The first Dominican Sisters had come to the newly formed diocese of Geraldton in Western Australia in 1899, at the invitation of Bishop W.B. Kelly. Cf. Ruth Marchant James, *Fields of Gold*, pp. 21-2.
2. A few days after she arrived with her family in Dublin, Sister Mary Declan (Lucy) Callaly suffered a stroke and died in Beaumount Hospital, Dublin.